from Chris Dan &
matt & Mike
Mother's Day 2002

Mothers &
Other Heroes
by Laura
Yulfer

Mothers & Other Heroes

by Laura Pulfer

ORANGE FRAZER *PRESS*
Wilmington, Ohio

ISBN 1-882203-60-7

Additional copies of *Mothers and Other Heroes* or other Orange Frazer Press publications may be ordered directly from:

Orange Frazer Press, Inc.
Box 214
37½ West Main Street
Wilmington, Ohio 45177

Telephone 1.800.852.9332 for price and shipping information
Web Site: www.orangefrazer.com

Cover illustration by Linda Scharf
Cover art by Margaret Hawley

Library of Congress Cataloging-in-Publication Data

Pulfer, Laura, 1946-
    Mothers and other heroes / by Laura Pulfer.
        p. cm.
    ISBN 1-882203-60-7 (alk. paper)
    I. Title.

PN4874.P79 A3 2001
814'.6--dc21

00-051682

To my husband, Mike,
one of the other heroes

And as always, for my mother,
Betty Rose Archer.
Every good thing I have done in my life
is because I looked first into her eyes
and saw that I could.

Table Of Contents

Acknowledgements

This book was Pete Johnson's idea. He's my editor at *The Cincinnati Enquirer* and—possibly because he is so thoroughly decent himself—believes that a good story is quite often a story about good. My thanks to him and to the unsung heroes at any newspaper in America, the copy desk. My own personal saviours include Gayle McCaskey, Kathy McDermott, Barrett Brunsman, Jim Calhoun and Paul Clark. If you find intolerable errors and gaudy excesses, you can be assured that I have circumvented their assistance and ignored their advice. Ray Zwick and Sally Besten of *The Enquirer's* library have never been too busy to help.

These stories appeared first in *The Enquirer* and are reprinted with permission.

Introduction

These are the stories I tell myself when I'm having a bad day.

Feeling blue? Wrap yourself in the goodness of Ruth Schmitt. Meet the thoroughly gallant Bonfield girls and the amazing Miz Ballew, celebrating her 102nd birthday with incredible verve. Learn the secret of life from Paula Howard. Let me introduce you to my utterly ruthless (and I mean this in a *good* way) mom and my aunts, relentless grime-fighters.

Get to know a nurse who regularly allows her patients to break her heart. Say hello to a young lawyer who wouldn't give up until he sprung an innocent man. And a police officer with a shattered hip who managed to get the bad guy and radio for help without—as her grandmother points out—saying any "bad words."

Worried about the next generation? Try the Irish cure. Or think about the boy with the blue hair. Come with me to a peaceful place where forty-eight little souls are generous proof that every human life has value.

Some of the people here are famous—Julia Child, Nikki Giovanni, Barry Larkin—but most are not. Most are simply people who have shown extraordinary grace or courage. Some have brilliant ideas. Or that rarest of all commodities—common sense. They let me suspect that I, too, might one day find something better, finer in myself than I imagined possible.

My heroes are funny and moving and brave. Sometimes they talked to me when they were in incredible pain. Sometimes they shamed me with their goodness. Sometimes they made me laugh.

Always, I was honored to be the typist.

Laura Pulfer
Cincinnati 2000

One

Cleanliness Is Next To Motherliness

Laura Pulfer

The Utterly Ruthless Mom

WHENEVER ANYONE ASKED, I told a harmless lie. "Are you hoping for a boy or a girl?"

And, as every good pregnant woman knows, there is only one permissible answer to that one. "We don't care as long as the baby is healthy." If you're lucky enough to be carrying a child, our reasoning goes, it would be shamefully greedy to be picky about its sex. And chauvinistic to hint that it matters. Even my mother, on that occasion, was politically correct.

It was the last time.

The truth is she wanted a girl. And when it was my turn, so did I. More than that, I wanted a girl who would feel the same way about me as I feel about my mother. After our daughter, Meg, was born, I asked my husband if he thought that she would love me as much as I love my mom. "Well, I don't know," he said. "But I'll bet she will love your mother as much as you do."

She does. Who could blame her? My mother taught my daughter how to paint her fingernails when she was 4 and how to drive when she was 13. They roller skated and jumped rope together. My mother gave Meg her cheesecake recipe and taught her how to use it. She pierced my daughter's ears and sent her encouraging notes when I had grounded her "for life."

Sure. Let me be the bad guy. "It's your turn," my mother said.

During my teen-age years, she was ruthless. A remorseless snoop. She knew the contents of all my drawers. "I was putting away your underwear and found a pack of cigarettes."

She read my diary. "It fell open."

And my personal mail. "I've fed that boy a hundred times. I consider him a mutual friend."

The ACLU would probably have helped me sue. Today's enlightened counselors would shake their heads over "privacy issues." She would stop at nothing. She was in league with my teachers. She conspired with my father. She made me go to Sunday school. She insisted that

I speak civilly to my elders even if they pinched my cheeks and asked impertinent questions.

She said things like, "You want a reason? Because I'm your mother and I say so." Hallmark has Mother's Day cards for everything else, but I couldn't find one that said thanks for being willing to do absolutely anything to keep me safe. Thanks for knowing that although we might be friends one day, you were willing to postpone it until I was an adult.

We are great friends now, my mother and I. And my other friend is my daughter, who thoughtfully supplied me with a granddaughter, Rosie. Just what we both wanted, although we didn't say so. When Meg was in the hospital, in labor, I distinguished myself by grabbing the nurse by the lapels and shrieking that I would give her a thousand dollars if she'd give Meg her epidural. Now. In fact, I may have said a thousand dollars and a new car. I don't remember. But it was not my finest hour.

My mother would have handled the situation with considerably more tact. Probably I will never have her finesse. Assuredly I will never have her style. My idea of well-groomed is when both my shoes match and my hem is not held up with masking tape. But I have learned the important lessons.

So far, I have taught Rosie how to turn on her mother's computer. I have hooked her on country music and gold jewelry. I am wondering how old she should be before we go out and get a tattoo together.

"My mother," says a friend, "drives me crazy."

I told her, "I know what you mean."

It is a harmless lie.

—*May 1999*

Laura Pulfer

Turkey, Yams And Lemon Pledge

IN MY FAMILY, the beginning of November is when you hear the starting gun for the Great Holiday Cleanup. Oh, not at my own, personal house. We're still finding plastic Easter eggs under the couch cushions. But this is crunch-time for my mom and my aunts, relentless grime-fighters.

These ladies—all of whom qualify for the senior rate when they go to the movies—could out-lunge, out-pump and out-aerobicize any woman at my gym. Free weights? They sling around forty-pound bags of water-softener salt and monster jugs of bottled water. Stairmasters? They climb real stairs fifty times a day with folded underwear and freshly ironed shirts. Rowing? They do the vacuum cleaner stroke. And reps with the mop.

They work out daily with their personal trainer, Mr. Clean. But the big dirt-a-thon is spring and fall.

Comfortably fixed, they could afford the services of some outfit like Maids R Us. But their standards are nearly impossible. These women regularly change their shelf paper, launder dog toys and alphabetize video tapes. Plus they cannot shake a lifetime of saying, "By the time I tell somebody else how to do it, I might as well do it myself."

They are a pragmatic mix of old-fashioned virtue and modern aids. One relative—let's call her Aunt Peggy—banished every last molecule of hair spray film from her bathroom, and now spritzes in the garage, primping in the sideview mirror of her car. Just until after the holidays.

Stories like this leave me weak with humility. It almost makes me want to clean my closets and throw away my prom dress. Almost. I believe that I have broken the cycle of cleanliness. Or maybe I just didn't get the scrubbing gene. Of course, truly accomplished housekeepers are not just born. My grandmother trained them. There were eight children, seven girls and Prince Charlie. My uncle, an excellent man in many respects, does not know which end of the mop is the handle.

Family photos show every little girl with a freshly ironed dress, shiny shoes and long curls. And this was before fabric softener and permanent press and hair gel. Grandma ran a tight ship. The older girls took care of the younger kids. And cleaned, supervised by Grandma, the mother of all housekeepers.

Saturday was cleaning day. "It was hell, if you want to know the truth," my mother says. "You started with bathrooms, and when you got good enough you worked your way up to something better." Legend has it that my Aunt Patty, possibly the most compulsive, strips to the buff and cleans her bathroom wearing only long rubber gloves and boots. But no one has ever seen this.

Wash day was slick with detergent and fragrant with bluing and bleach. Clothes were fed through a hand wringer, and tough stains attacked on the washboard. My grandmother's wash line was the envy of the neighborhood, with everything hung in sequence and by category—underwear out of sight in the middle.

Women like these were never simply excellent housekeepers. It wasn't really about keeping their houses. It was about their families. We were never told we couldn't play in the house or forbidden to bring home our messy and noisy friends. Bright and energetic, they were not encouraged to "work outside the home" but were destined to be very good at whatever work there was. During the war, some became Rosie the Riveters. But, naturally, they surrendered their jobs when the men returned.

On Thanksgiving Day, every one of my aunties sits around a table, surrounded by her children. And her children's children. If you asked them right then what they are thankful for, they'd probably say Sara and Hank and Janet and David and Thom and Becky and George.

But I'll bet if you had asked them at the beginning of the month, they'd have said Pledge and Windex and Tide and Spic 'n Span and Comet.

—November 1997

It's Beginning To Smell A Lot Like Christmas

MORE THAN MUSIC, more than words even, smells bring back memories. Evocative, the shrinks call it. Aromatherapy, the pseudo-shrinks call it. For instance, the scent of old-fashioned laundry bluing could put me right at my mother's feet while she wrestles with an old wringer washer in our basement in 1951. One whiff of chalk, and I'm banging erasers after school in Miss Mayer's class. Talking out of turn again.

Christmas smells like pine, of course. That wonderful Christmas-tree aroma that surprises you on dark mornings when you've forgotten it's there. Before you see it. Not the acrid odor of those year-round phoney pine smells, the ones in cleaning liquids or hanging from the rear-view mirrors of cars. Who decided we wanted all our possessions to smell like pine or lemons? The smell of lemon is good. On a lemon. But not on your furniture or your floor or in your car. Same with pine, in my opinion. And cedar.

Do you know they sell blocks of cedar for your underwear drawer? I guess this is in case you would like to smell like a hamster. You also can smell like a raspberry or a giant vanilla bean if you use certain beauty products. Smelling like a person, apparently, just won't do.

Improving on smells is probably one of the earliest Christmas traditions, when you think about it. The three Wise Men showed up at the manger bearing gold, frankincense and myrrh. The last two are fragrant resins from certain trees that grow in Africa and Asia. I do not know what they smell like, but probably better than a manger. And certainly better than a lemon.

Our Christmas tree this year was particularly fragrant. Sometimes I stood next to it just to breathe its goodness. And also to inventory the presents underneath, wishing there really was a Santa who did the shopping and delivered everything for the price of a couple of cookies and a glass of milk. This reminded me of—evoked, you might say—the pre-knowing-about-Santa days and another holiday fragrance: Ajax.

It could smell like lemons today, but when I was 6 years old, Ajax smelled like cleanser. A nice, honest, slightly unpleasant signal that your sinks, toilets and bathtubs had been attended. My mom was scouring the tub when I got home from school that day. It was Christmas Eve, and we'd just had our second-grade Christmas party.

At the party was Sandra Newcomer, a notable troublemaker. Three years later she would be the first one of us to wear—and to genuinely need—a bra. So you can see how hateful she could be. Anyway, she told me Santa was a hoax. "Your parents buy all the stuff," she said with a sneer. My brother, Steven, and I had already discussed this and decided that if the stuff came from our parents, we would be getting coats and mittens and pyjamas instead of bicycles and cowboy guns and roller skates. So, I ran into the bathroom and asked Mom. She sat me on the edge of the tub and told me about the little girl in 1897 who asked the same question. "Yes, Virginia, there is a Santa Claus," was the reply from the *New York Sun*. Mom's version contained considerably less information about "fairies dancing on the lawn" and "external light" of childhood than the original.

But it certainly captured the wonder of my normally practical mom and dad, conniving to buy us all kinds of frivolous and expensive gifts. For absolutely no credit whatsoever. Just because they loved us.

So, for me, Christmas aromatherapy is pine with just a hint of Ajax.

—*December 1999*

Laura Pulfer

Two

A Sparkle In The Public Eye

Laura Pulfer

The Joy Of Not Cooking With Julia

JULIA CHILD FIGURED OUT about five seconds into our conversation that it would be an unhappy exercise in futility to try to talk about cooking. So we didn't. This was a very big relief for us both. She was spared my recipe for Twinkies Flambe. And I was spared the humiliation of trying to act as though I would voluntarily eat the pancreas of a calf.

Her voice sounds exactly as it does on television, a cultured yodel. Flawlessly groomed, she has lovely blue eyes, undimmed by her 86 years. When she went to her sixtieth class reunion at Smith College, she had a terrible time. "Everybody was old and let their hair go gray and didn't wear any makeup. I hated it. I'm never going back to another one."

She may cook like the French, but she is a genuine American treasure. Unself-conscious, curious, intellectually quick. In 1990, she came to Cincinnati to raise money for Planned Parenthood after its original building was bombed. While here, she visited the controversial Mapplethorpe exhibit at the Contemporary Art Center, making her way into the building through a group of protesters who so annoyed her that she reserved for them her ultimate curse. She wished them a life filled with margarine. She has a continuing feud with what she calls the "nutrition police" and once said, "Anything that says 'healthy' I stay away from. Giving up butter, for instance, means that in about two years, you will be covered in dandruff." Not wishing to be covered in dandruff and also wishing to please her, I slathered butter on everything that came my way during dinner. Her advice is to simply eat less of better stuff.

"I think parents should be teaching their children self-discipline," she said. "Don't take big pieces of cake. Exercise. It is really horrible to look at these great big bubble butts. I think: How are you going to get rid of that now?"

Bubble butts?

"Julia is never trying to be funny," says a friend. "She is just being herself." Herself is the distinctive voice that taught America to cook. As author Albert Pyle says, she is "the woman

who rescued her homeland from the tyranny of meatloaf and molded salads."

Maybe you spent time with her in front of a black-and-white television in the 1960s when she was starting her PBS series, *The French Chef.* Or maybe you conquered your fear of soufflés with her cookbooks.

Maybe you saw her on Letterman's show, where she was not only more likeable than Dave but considerably funnier. Maybe you remember the wickedly hilarious impersonation by Dan Aykroyd on Saturday Night Live. Someone asked her whether she had given Mr. Aykroyd acting lessons. Without hesitation, she leaned forward and did a perfect imitation of Dan Aykroyd imitating Julia Child.

Under the relentless eye of the television camera for more than thirty-five years, she has been revealed to us as an extraordinary and substantial woman. One of a kind. A gifted teacher. A Technicolor personality.

The food, if I may say so, is incidental.

—November 1998

N i k k i ' s   P o e t r y   I s   N o t   F o r   S i s s i e s

MY FRIENDS KNOW I'd rather watch Seinfeld reruns than improve my mind. Nice people, they refuse to give up. I am warmed by the memory of Susan pawing through her purse during a particularly tiresome lecture. She found a cherry LifeSaver with hardly any lint on it and passed it down the row to me.

"Now, shut up," she said graciously.

But of course I never do, grumbling at each new effort to expand my intellectual horizons.

"There's somebody I want you to meet, my friend Deidra said fifteen years ago. "She's a poet."

Oh, boy. That should be a lot of fun. Maybe we can order lunch in iambic pentameter. "She's not that kind of poet," Deidra said.

And she's not. She is Nikki Giovanni.

For thirty years, she has been the exquisitely angry voice of black America, the woman the *New York Times* calls the "Princess of Black Poetry." Now, the *Washington Post* says she's a "venerable lioness." When, I wondered, did she get to be venerable? Only yesterday we were worrying about our kids, wondering how they'd turn out, laughing through a cigarette haze. Her son, Thomas, now is an attorney with a very fancy New York law firm.

She was, even then, rather famous. But not rich. She lived with her mother and taught some very lucky students at the College of Mount St. Joseph. I got to know her well enough to let her beat me at tennis. (This would not be her version.) When she was diagnosed with lung cancer four years ago, I pushed my way into her hospital room when she was still woozy, pestering her doctor for reassurances.

I do not kid myself, pretending I am a large part of her life, but she is a significant part of mine. She has told me things that I could not hear from anybody else, that I would not hear from anybody else. She has taught white-bread me something about being black in America.

Since she moved to Virginia to teach English to more lucky college students, we have rarely spoken. But she generously passes along her thoughts at least every other year with a new book. She's touring with her latest, *Blues for All the Changes,* and we met for lunch. Nikki has been playing with her hair. It's in close, blond ringlets. She wears a blue, oxford cloth shirt, with a man's tie knotted loosely at the open neck. She looks good. Healthy?

"Yes," she says. "All clear."

Her plan, she says, is to negotiate a truce with her cancer. "I'd like an agreement that we will live together for another thirty years."

She has an opinion about everything. Her poetry is by turns a rant and a love story. Always instructive. Never boring. Beautifully metered.

There is talk now about a national dialogue on race. That's probably a good idea, very enlightening. My friends will sign up for the lecture series. Myself, I prefer to have this conversation with somebody who can give me a great big dose of education without candy.

—*June 1999*

Remembering Jackie's Boy

HE WAS A 38-YEAR-OLD MAN. Can that be? Well, of course, we know that John F. Kennedy Jr. was not a child. We have watched him from his baby days in the White House, playing with his mother's fake pearls and under his father's desk.

We realize he had grown up. Lord knows we have had every opportunity to see it in living color and black and white headlines. "Hunk Flunks" was the ungenerous notice of his first attempt to pass the New York bar exam. "The Sexiest Man Alive," crowed People magazine. Still, we appear to be surprised. Like a maiden aunt at a family reunion, America seemed to want to pinch this young man's cheek and exclaim at the passage of time.

We can picture the Kennedy compound. Most of us can recite with some fidelity the names and circumstances of previous Kennedy family tragedies. We have seen the white Masses. We can guess which cousins will be selected to be pall bearers. We know them by name and have seen them in similar circumstances. Many times. Where is Caroline, we wondered anxiously, as news unfolded of the missing plane, the search.

We recognize the names on the maps, tracing the doomed flight, the search area. Edgartown. Chappaquiddick. Hyannis. And now Gay Head. Reporters staking out the Cape Cod home of the late Rose Kennedy probably know exactly where the phone hookups might be. At newspapers, there is no dearth of photographs of this young man, the best-looking of all the Kennedys, male and female. ABC's Barbara Walters talked about when "my daughter and I were at the Kennedy home." NBC anchor Tom Brokaw spoke about the "good relationship" he shared with John Kennedy Jr. CBS's Dan Rather choked up on the air.

Occasionally, somebody would remember guiltily that another family has suffered an anguishing double loss. But the thing is, we don't know the Bessettes. This was John-John. We liked this kid. We admired the way he managed to sidestep the drugs and scandals that appeared to be the modern-day Kennedy curse. For that, he credited his mother. "I always grew up just living a fairly normal life," he told *USA Today*. A normal life. Bless his heart. He couldn't possibly have known what a normal life was all about. There have been the inevitable comparisons to the death of Princess Diana. But it is not the same. Not at all. We met Diana when she was a young woman, a bride. We have known JFK Jr. from birth. The way we feel about him is more like the way we feel about Diana's children—particularly Wills—than the way we felt about her.

We Americans have strong maternal and paternal instincts. Our children who are of an age with John Kennedy Jr. and with Prince William may see the sadness, the waste. But an older generation will take it harder, the generation who can remember "where I was" when the news of another death came out of Dallas. We will not be thinking of the man he worked to become, the affable guy with a wife and a future.

We are mourning Jackie's beautiful little boy.

—July 1999

The Unexpurgated  Bobbie Sterne

HAS THE OFFICIAL GUSHING STOPPED? Is it time to talk about the real Bobbie Sterne? The one who locks her keys in her car with alarming regularity? The one who owns a bright yellow jumpsuit and gold boots?

Since she quietly exited Cincinnati City Council, we have heard all about her contributions to our city. But not once has anyone mentioned her chocolate habit. Or her racy car. Or the fact that she is a closet daredevil —para-sailing, camping in a yurt. Not ten years ago. Now.

Dignified. Principled. Gallant. And fun. Sometimes even funny.

She loves telling about sitting in her 1978 silver Corvette, a one-owner car, meticulously maintained, recently repainted, stick shift, fast. Two kids came by, looked appreciatively, then noted with disgust that "some old lady was driving it."

Well, by anybody's standards, this is certainly some old lady. She'll be 78 in November.

And for twenty-five of those years, she has been a public servant. A real one. She is the politician who shows up at church suppers and not-so-grand openings and funerals and weddings. She'll say a few words, if asked, but mostly she listens, standing patiently with her aching, narrow feet neatly shod in Ferragamo pumps and holding her ever-present handbag. Just like Queen Elizabeth, she's never without her purse.

I don't know what the queen keeps in hers—probably biscuits for those miserable Corgis—but Mrs. Sterne carries the basics: her calendar, lipstick, a wallet. Oh, and possibly— OK, probably—a Reese's peanut-butter cup. The woman is a chocoholic, not a recovering one. Active. Practicing. I'll bet if you looked in her freezer right now, all you'd find is frozen candy bars, coffee and Graeter's ice cream with some kind of chip. She's not choosy about the flavor, as she thinks the mint or the mocha is just there to suspend the chocolate.

Lunch is wheat crackers with peanut butter and Diet Coke. Dinner is often rubber chicken. Her calendar is a horror, brutally full. Her normal day is ten to twelve hours. Every day. "People asked her to a lot of events, birthdays, anniversaries," an aide says, "and she thinks they really wanted her to come." So she went. The thing is, she was not there for a photo op. And she probably already had their votes.

Picking up votes isn't at the top of her agenda. She has never been afraid of unpopular issues—gay rights, abortion, unions, minority recruitment. In fact, she's generally unafraid. Her bravery is habitual and long-standing. Last October, when a man crept into her home through a window, Mrs. Sterne tried to push him back out. He grabbed her, put her in a headlock and took a billfold. She went out campaigning the same night and was at work the next day.

I don't suppose some two-bit thug was much of a threat after the battlefield. "When Japan invaded Manchuria," she said, "I remember saying to people, "Why are you sitting here? Why don't you stop them?" By then, she'd finished nurse's training, having earned tuition by cleaning houses and baby sitting to get there. "After Pearl Harbor, it was automatic that I was going."

In a mobile hospital unit, she arrived in France, climbing from the troop carrier down a rope to a beach being strafed. From there, she was sent to Leage, Belgium, where "the enemy was buzz-bombing the place constantly."

No wonder she handled the potshots and bickering from some of her council colleagues with such equanimity. "Brats," she called them sometimes. And she was the one who provided adult supervision.

It's her official life that makes us so respectful, gushy even. The other stuff—the endless chicken dinners, the reliable goodness, unexpected bravery, the fast car, the chocolate— merely makes us love her.

—*July 1998*

M V P   B a r r y   L a r k i n ' s   B e s t   C o a c h

IF YOU'VE BEEN WONDERING how Barry Larkin got to be the National League's Most Valuable Player, I think I went bowling with her.

Actually, that's stretching a point quite a bit. Shirley Larkin, Barry's mom, bowls in a league, and I hung out with her and asked her nosy questions between frames. She was wearing a white T-shirt with hot pink letters that said "Number 1 Fan." She asked Velva Sheen to print "Number 1 Fan of Barry Larkin," but was told that the Reds own the rights to that.

"Think of that," she says, "his own mother." I was still trying to imagine somebody refusing to do something she told them to do. And I couldn't.

Friendly, attractive, engaging, direct. For want of a less pretentious word, let's call her charismatic. "She's the spark plug," says a friend. "Her husband, Robert, is the quiet one."

She bowls a pretty good game, puts the ball down softly, plays it straight. No hook, no fancy pin action. She says her children get their extraordinary physical gifts from their father. Her game is bingo. Her best game this day is 174. Her average is 146. I think I brought her luck.

When she comes back to where I'm sitting, she picks up our conversation right where it left off. She has concentration. So, she says, does Barry. "When he was little, he was stubborn," she says. Properly channeled, it became determination.

It was that channeling stuff I wanted to know about. Barry Larkin is not just a superior

athlete. He's a good guy. With class. An overachiever. Just like his brothers and sister. How did they get that way?

"People have been asking us that for years," Shirley says. "All I can tell you is that the only way we could survive with all those kids is to have rules. Daddy and I were boss. And we spanked them, if we needed to. We didn't need to very often."

The first four kids were each thirteen months apart, and Stephen, the baby, was "our surprise" eight years after Byron Larkin, who now is a financial planner, was born. The oldest, Mary Robin, works as a chemist and is studying to be a dentist. Michael is a sports promoter, and Stephen plays for the Reds' farm system.

And Barry is at the top of his game.

He's good. Has always been good; could hook slide when he was a year old. "He was a natural," his mother says. A "pretty good" student, he flunked Latin in the seventh grade at Walnut Hills High School, so Shirley and Robert Larkin pulled him off the basketball team. "It just didn't work. He was a much better student when he was playing a sport. Sometimes I think that's what parents don't do—notice what works for their child. They're just not all the same."

Before long, all the Larkin children were in athletics. Robert, a chemist for the National Institute for Occupational Safety and Health, and Shirley had five times the usual pickup, delivery and spectator duties. "But no matter what, the family always had dinner together. Even if it was at 10 o'clock at night."

The house in Silverton, where Byron and Barbara Larkin live now with their two kids, was a neighborhood gathering place. "I didn't mind the noise and the mess," Shirley says. "I always wanted to know where my children were."

Once a neighbor complained to Robert about some bare spots on the lawn. "One of the spots was first base," Shirley says, rolling her eyes. "Robert told the man he'd rather raise children than grass."

OK. So here's the secret of the Larkin family success from the spokesmother: Parenting is a team sport.

—*November 1995*

Laura Pulfer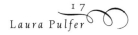

A Temporary Tribute To Albert Sabin

IF YOU'RE ABOUT MY AGE, you can remember polio. You can remember your mom saying you couldn't swim because you might get a chill. Doctors wouldn't take your tonsils out during polio season, between May and October. Kids in clunky metal and leather leg braces. Maybe you even remember an iron lung.

That was the worst. These huge metal tubes were a peculiar sickly green with portholes in the sides and a mirror over the victim's face. The machine made an unmistakable rhythmic and chilling whoosh.

It's easy to forget that there are still thirty thousand who survived my generation's most dreaded childhood disease. Most of them have thrown away the braces and learned to use weakened hands and arms.

Radio personality Jim Scott had polio when he was 12. "I remember my left arm feeling funny, tingly." That was the beginning of months of rehabilitation and an arm that still is partially disabled. He was sitting on his bed in a clinic in upstate New York when he heard that a vaccine had been discovered.

He met Dr. Sabin in 1987 at the dedication of the Albert B. Sabin Convention Center. "It really was a sweet moment. He took hold of my left hand that, of course, I thought was so unusual, so unique. And I realized that he had seen thousands of hands like mine."

We love to brag that the man who saved billions of lives around the world belongs to us. He developed the polio vaccine in the early 1950s while doing research for the University of Cincinnati Medical Center. Since 1977, there has been a park named for him, a tiny patch of green with a couple of benches on Third Street between Plum and Elm streets.

Owned by the Ohio Department of Transportation, it was maintained by the city park board, more a decorated right of way than a park. Now heavy equipment is parked there, the name removed. This tribute to Dr. Sabin was not only small but temporary. And this was the man called the Patron Saint of Mothers.

Although I'm sure fathers worried about polio, too, mothers were on the front lines of this disease. The "Mothers' March" collected dimes, back when you could still actually buy something with one of them.

One mother I remember, Mrs. Beery, learned how to play the piano so she could teach her son when he got home from the hospital. Doctors had said he'd never use his left hand again. She was determined that he would. And he did.

I remember a church picnic when the Doty brothers weren't allowed to swim with the rest of us because their mom was afraid they'd catch it. They caught it anyway, and wore braces on their legs through high school.

A girl caught the worst stuff, bulbar polio and spent the rest of her life in an iron lung. She learned how to "frog breathe" so she could escape the lung for brief, giddy moments with her friends.

Dr. Albert Sabin is the one who made machines like hers obsolete. And the little patch of land named for him was never a grand enough sign of our gratitude.

It will be replaced—sort of—by the new and improved Fort Washington Way, absorbed into a "multipurpose, pedestrian-friendly space," says John Deatrick, an engineer with the city. He promised better green space, with lots of big trees and walkways and benches. He showed me drawings, and it looked pretty good.

But it won't be named for Dr. Albert Sabin.

So when you're walking down a twenty-eight-foot-wide boulevard on Third Street from Broadway to Plum Street, in shade provided by trees instead of buildings, take a big breath of air. Notice that your kids are walking without crutches, breathing without the whoosh of the iron lung.

Maybe Dr. Sabin would think that's tribute enough.

—*July 1998*

Three

Practical Magic And Professional Services

Blame Kevin If You Are Laughing Less

KEVIN BREWER SURE TAKES all the fun out of lawyer jokes.

A lawyer driving his big BMW crashes into a tree, totaling the car. "My BMW," he screams in anguish. When the ambulance arrives, one of the medics gasped, "His left arm is gone." The attorney sobbed, "Oh, no. My Rolex."

A lawyer for less than two years who drives a five-year-old Nissan, Kevin is the guy responsible for freeing a man who served ten years in prison on a rape charge. The victim has said since 1992 that the wrong man was in jail. Nobody paid any attention. Except Kevin.

A West Side boy who naturally names his parish when asked where he grew up, he is a product of St. Xavier High School and UC law school. He is also, not incidentally, the product of his mother, Elaine McGuire, a vice president with TriHealth. Widowed when Kevin was 4, Elaine "tried to do the best I could as a single parent." She later married Frank McGuire, who is pleased to claim Kevin as his son. And vice versa.

An attorney presents himself to St. Peter at the Pearly Gates. "I'm only 49 years old. I'm too young to be dead." St. Peter consults his records and says, "That's odd. According to the hours you've billed, you're 119."

Johnny Reeves had been convicted in 1989 of the rape of his 8-year-old cousin, and the court was considering his status as a sexual predator. Just housekeeping, really. Mr. Reeves had forty more years to serve and was not scheduled for a probation hearing.

Kevin Brewer was provided with the case number and a court date, less than three weeks away. He would be paid $30 an hour and allowed to spend up to three hours. He pawed through the file, then went to microfilm for more information, unearthing an affidavit from the victim recanting her original statement.

Many hours later, he found evidence that the victim's father was being investigated for the crime when he hanged himself.

Q: Why have scientists begun to use lawyers instead of lab rats for research?

A: They are more plentiful and researchers don't get attached to them.

The first question Johnny Reeves asked his new court-appointed attorney was, "Do you know anything about my case?" Kevin did. By the time he finally met face to face with his client, he had traced the victim and gotten her to agree to come to court. The next day, after hearing her testimony, the judge released Mr. Reeves.

Q: How many lawyers does it take to change a light bulb?

A: None. They'd rather keep their clients in the dark.

Kevin says this case "kinda reminds you of the importance of being thorough." Naturally, I'm trying to get him to be as giddy as I would be under the same circumstances. He will say only, "I'm glad I could help him out. I look at him and think, 'Just a few days ago he was living in a box. What if I'd just blown it off, not followed up?'"

The next time I hear one of those lawyer jokes, I will think of Kevin Brewer, who could have put in his three hours, collected his $90 and allowed an innocent man to spend another forty years in jail. I will imagine his wide blue eyes, trying to focus on hazy microfilm and his hand, which could have been wrapped around a nine iron, wrapped instead around a telephone receiver. Calling strangers, refusing to give up, refusing to accept a runaround. I will remember his earnest young face, his cowlick and what he told his mother when he had his very first court case.

"He is counting on me, Mom."

And so are we all, Kevin.

—*July 1999*

Report From The Trenches
Of The Drug War

JAMES J. SLATTERY, PUBLIC DEFENDER AND RECOVERING ALCOHOLIC, tells a very convincing story. And it comes with a picture.

He's a big guy, about two hundred twenty-five pounds and three inches or so over six feet tall. At 52, he has an enviable head of reddish-blond hair, neatly trimmed. Clear hazel eyes. Nice suit, good tie, white shirt. The picture of prosperity.

The other picture is a photograph of Jim at 146 pounds, taken five years ago. He had lost everything. His family, a house in Indian Hill. A sailboat. His car had been repossessed. His license to practice law had been suspended.

Oh, and he was dying.

"Toward the end, I was drinking a quart a day," he says. "Vodka." He woke up one day at 4 a.m., fully dressed in his car in a parking lot.

"I didn't know where I was," he says. "I looked up and saw a Big Bear sign, and I knew we didn't have those stores around here. I was in Columbus, and I had no idea how I'd gotten there."

He jumped out of his car and ran around it, looking for signs that he might have hit something—or somebody. "I was terrified."

But he still wasn't finished drinking.

Finally in July of 1994, his liver rebelled. Just shut down. Doctors told him that he had a fifty percent chance of living another two years. He dried out temporarily and moved in with his father in Chicago.

But he still wasn't finished drinking.

His father threw him out, telling his son: "I love you. I can't stop you from drinking, but I don't have to watch you die." Jim picked up a bottle on his way out of town. The five-hour drive took him five days.

Mothers and Other Heroes

"I had burned every bridge I had."

He arrived in Cincinnati too drunk to qualify for the VA Hospital's detox program. He checked himself into University Hospital's psych unit. Then back to the VA Hospital, where "they saved my life."

He lived for three years at Prospect House, a men's substance abuse center in Price Hill, and says his work with addicts and other alcoholics "reminds me of how grateful I need to be." He tells his story whenever he is asked, "without trying to make myself look good."

So we will leave that to someone else.

"You just can't believe what he does with people," says Judge Deidra Hair of Hamilton County's Drug Court, where he works as a public defender. "They can't con him. He has been there. They know that. And he really cares about people."

They know that too.

Jim Slattery remembers a day recently when he sat across the table from a client, an addict. "He was a tough kid," Jim rumbles in a voice so deep it is almost a growl. "He had on his street face, ready to meet the world."

The lawyer says he leaned forward and lowered his voice, pulled the kid toward him. "I know you're scared," he said. And the big man rumbled on for a few minutes, telling his very convincing story and watching for a reaction.

Finally, tears began to roll. And at that moment, they both—the street tough in baggy pants and the affable man in a suit—looked at each other and saw all the wonderful and terrible possibilities.

—*January 1999*

Laura Pulfer

Miracles Of St. Joseph
Are Available To All

"IN A WAY," THE WOMAN SAYS, opening the door to the classroom, "they are perfect little beings."

Six children cluster around their teacher. They are completely silent, their wheelchairs locked in place, their heads lolling. The teacher casually suctions fluid from a tube in the throat of a little boy on her left. Music. This is their music lesson.

It seems to me an exercise in wishful thinking.

We are at St. Joseph Home in Sharonville. The residents are, in the words of a brochure, children and young adults who have "profound mental and physical disabilities. All are nonverbal and nonambulatory."

The teacher beats a drum.

"You like that, don't you, Mimi?"

No response.

Wishful thinking.

Then I notice that Joey's tongue—his *tongue*—is moving in time to the music.

The teacher puts her hands over his, and together they make music on the drum. His eyes snap open. They lock with mine. And he gives an achingly beautiful smile.

Mimi nudges a device strapped to the back of her chair that makes a rhythmic noise in response to the music. She is fully engaged. I am simply too unsophisticated to see it. But I am beginning to see, guided gently by Sister Marianne Van Vurst, the administrator of St. Joseph, who has opened the door to me. And my eyes.

After a while, I do not see the wheelchairs. I see little kids. Every shoelace is tied. They are dressed in spotless knit shirts, sweat shirts, corduroy jeans. How much time must it take to dress each child? And to dress each child several times a day? Accidents happen.

There are forty-eight children who live here. The Sisters of Charity who operate St.

Joseph do thirty loads of laundry—twenty-five pounds per load—every day. Spotless. And fragrant with fabric softener.

As I stroke Mimi's chubby arm, run my fingers across her dimpled hand, I notice something. "Look, Sweetie," I say, "your nail polish matches your outfit today."

With some pride, Sister Lynn Heper tells me that it always does. "That's important to Mimi." Sister Lynn would know that because she carried Mimi, 4, "in my arms" to St. Joseph when the little girl was only three weeks old.

Beating the drum, brushing their teeth, making Christmas ornaments, finger painting. Much of this is accomplished with four hands, adult hands over little ones.

"How come the Lord let you stay here?" Sister Charlotte says she asks each time she meets a new child. "And then we try to find out what is unique about this angel." That's what she calls them. There is an official Hall of Angels with photographs.

She points to Trevor, who was able to pick up a cup and knew how to give a hug.

In his room, Carlos sprawls blissfully, listening to opera. Some of the other kids like country music. Some like rap. The women are vigilant, alert. Whatever these children appear to need, they will try to provide.

Quality of life? These children are not merely cared for. They are treasured. They have, of course, a full range of emotions, including joy. And, I presume, frustration and anger, although I did not see it. But they have no hatred. There's no deceit, no conniving, no malice of any kind. This is not the real world.

The real world is an incomprehensible—if not suspicious—war. It is a Constitutional crisis occasioned by unspeakable selfishness. If you would like some relief from the real world, you may come to St. Joseph. They need people to sew name tags on clothing, to help with field trips, to do laundry, to read to the children.

It's peaceful there. And tangible and generous proof that every human life has value. It is, in a way, the perfect place for an exercise in wishful thinking.

—*December 1998*

Draw On SCPA Teacher For Inspiration

HENRY GLOVER THINKS WE ARE GOING TO TALK about his remarkable attendance record. And, I suppose, we are. At least at first.

It is a noteworthy accomplishment, the kind that probably will appear in the Guinness Book of Records some day. Friday, he will complete fifty-seven years of school without missing a single day.

Not one. Zip. Zero.

When he wasn't going to school, he was teaching school. His perfect record began in kindergarten in Morehead, Ky., and continued through college and graduate school.

His string will end at the School for Creative and Performing Arts, where he teaches painting and drawing. He guesses this is an unbroken skein of more than ten thousand, five hundred days.

But he has done something more than just show up for work.

"This may sound kind of dramatic," SCPA Principal Jeff Brokamp says, "but Hank has saved lives."

An art teacher? "Hank believed in the importance of the teacher-student relationship. He fought for kids. Kids knew they could depend on him. And so could I."

Drawing a straight line is fine if you can make a living with it. But what if you don't have the talent to be an artist? "Everyone should study art," Hank says firmly.

You might have a good time with your charcoal. You might create something pleasing to the eye, but you can't send a kid out into the world expecting his art class to help him with anything important. You know, like managing a stock portfolio or putting a Ford Explorer in the garage. Right?

"Art," he tells me politely, "helps a kid to think." Furthermore, he says most of what we know is based on what we see. Especially kids. And Henry Glover allowed them to see a man who came to work every day, who took his job—and them—seriously.

And what if you can teach kids that when somebody says they'll be someplace, they will? And what if you can teach kids that they should show up for work every day? "I was never sick, so I never took a sick day. It wouldn't have been honest."

Plus, he says, he might have missed something. Parents weighing "quality" time with their children against other demands in their lives might want to think about his example. Perhaps Mr. Glover's record—when considered with his accomplishments—can remind us of something very basic.

Sometimes helping kids begins simply with being there.

—*May 1999*

Wanted: New Doctor For Cranky Patient

BAD NEWS ARRIVED IN THE MAIL. Terrible news, really. One of my doctors is retiring. Worse, he is my gynecologist.

(Note to male readers: I will not be discussing the clinical aspects of our relationship, so you may continue to read without fear of finding out more than you want to know about stirrups and paper gowns. You can remain blessedly ignorant of what the medical instruction "scoot" means to the women in your lives.)

The official letter from Harold E. Johnstone, M.D., read:

"After thirty-four years in private practice and delivering more than five thousand babies, it is time for me to retire."

Geez, I noticed a little gray in his hair, but I picked this guy because he was young. And because I heard he took only difficult cases. Since I get cranky when I'm sick and tear coupons out of the magazines in the waiting room, I figured I qualified.

He delivered our daughter, Meg, twenty-four years ago, and I remember thinking I was glad the first voice she would hear was his. Soft. Gentle. He says I should check with some of the residents he has trained. Maybe I'd get a different impression.

And I expect he might not always be gentle with them.

He is sending them out on the difficult mission of keeping women healthy, sometimes with little cooperation from us. Once, when I missed my annual checkup, he called me himself.

"If you're seeing somebody else, that's fine," he told me tactfully. "I just wanted to make sure you're being cared for."

The truth is that I hadn't made an appointment for my mammogram—such an inconvenience—and I knew he would nag me. He did. So I got one. And it was his gentle voice—the one that ushered my daughter into this world—that told me I had breast cancer.

Other doctors, a surgeon and an oncologist, took over from there. But Dr. Johnstone called the hospital twice after I had surgery—"just to see how you're doing." I told him he sounded like he was calling from the bottom of a barrel. He was, he said, on vacation. Out of the country.

A very nice man.

There have been those times when all that he could do for one of us, all that modern medicine could do, has failed. And then, I have known him to put his head in is hands and cry like a baby.

He says he tells his residents it's important that they're smart and learn their specialty, that they develop the technical skills they need. "But your patient is the last one to know how good you are. You have to let them know you care about them."

Not too long ago, I had a scare, something that didn't look right, something that required another test. When he told me everything was OK, I said, "I knew you were worried."

He looked startled.

"Don't worry, Doctor. You haven't lost your game face. I just know you too well."

And he knows me.

This is something the new age of health care is going to have to factor into the equation. Every bean is the same to the bean counters. But we patients are not so tidy and uniform. Sometimes our complaints are embarrassing. We don't want to talk about them with a stranger.

Sometimes when we are cranky, it's because we're scared. And sometimes, even though we don't say a word, our doctor knows something is wrong because he knows how we look when we're healthy and happy. That takes time. And more than five minutes with an HMO doctor *du jour*.

So, Dr. Johnstone, I don't mind telling you that I am sincerely honked off that you are

unhooking yourself from your pager to go bird-watching. You will hand me off, I know, to another doctor you trust. I hope it's somebody young because I'm planning to be around for a long time.

Thanks to you.

—June 1999

Want To Fight? Here's An Angel Who Will Help

I WENT TO A FUNERAL LAST WEEK. Another one. Breast cancer.

She was a tiny little thing, and I often marveled at her fierce determination to stay alive. Funny and kind, with a laugh I will hear for the rest of my life, she was a nurse and gardener. In other words, an equal-opportunity caretaker.

Her friends gathered to pay their respects, to try to comfort her family, to listen to a summary of her life. The last part included state-of-the-art medical tortures—surgery, chemotherapy, radiation, bone marrow transplant, transfusions, drugs of every description. She took it all and went back for more, grateful to try something new, something that might work.

We were wondering—as you often do at times like this—if there was something more we might have done.

It made me think of another nurse.

Rita Sauer works in the office of Dr. Donna Stahl, a distinguished surgeon specializing in breast disease. Full disclosure here: Donna Stahl is my doctor, and Rita has seen me in a flimsy gown with a vent in an inconvenient place. She lets me take off my rings, shoes, jacket, and blow my nose before I step onto the scales. She insisted that I would live when I was afraid I would die.

This woman is not a casual acquaintance.

And I am sure that all her patients feel the same way. We are not just her job. Considering that many of us lose the fight, it must be terrible for her.

Laura Pulfer

"It makes me angry," she says. "Day in and day out, you see people who are scared, are fighting. This is not just any disease. This is really awful. I see women being so brave. And I just wanted to do something."

The "something" is a little angel, a chubby cherub, five inches tall. Made of cast colorless resin, he holds the signal breast cancer pink ribbon. He's very cute. And Rita thinks you should go out and buy him immediately.

Sales fund breast cancer research. Well, how much of the profits actually go to fight cancer? "All of it," Rita says firmly.

It would be very tidy and maybe flattering to insist that Rita is an angel, too. But I am remembering that once, during an office visit, she ambushed me with a squirt gun filled with disappearing ink. And angels don't have freckles, do they?

No, I don't think she is superhuman or mythic or heavenly. I just think she is an uncommonly good person, a nurse brave enough to let her patients break her heart. She walks about twenty miles a week, when "I think about them, people I've lost, their families."

A friend advised her to keep more distance. "But," she says, "I'm afraid of what I might miss."

There is a growing crowd of people with broken hearts. Not just women with breast cancer, but their kids and husbands and parents and partners. And nurses and doctors. We are beginning to know one another. We assemble with alarming frequency at the hospitals, the fund raisers, the funerals.

I think about Rita on her walks, reviewing her memories, hearing the echoes of laughter. I wonder how many times she has sat in one of those uncomfortable chairs, amid the aroma of flowers. Terrible. Sad. But at least she will not have to wonder if she could have done more.

—*March 1998*

Four

Lasting Impressions And Mild Insurrections

33
Laura Pulfer

A Tale Of Two Women, Jewels And A Fur Coat

HER HUSBAND WANTED HER TO HAVE A FUR COAT. Mink, he said. She protested, mildly, as women of her generation would do. She didn't need, didn't want one. He insisted, put the money into her hands.

It was 1924, and the woman's name was Rose Palm, nee Bast. Catholic, born and raised in Price Hill, she showed a little stubborn streak. Her children were raised, and she was in her 70s. "I've gotten along fine for all these years without a mink coat," she told her daughter.

So she took the money and spent it on a window.

It is the second stained-glass window on the left as you enter the doors of St. Francis De Sales Church at Madison Road and Woodburn Avenue in East Walnut Hills. About thirty feet high, the scene shows the youthful Jesus with the Pharisees.

Eventually, Mr. Palm noticed that the money was gone but his wife was still wearing a cloth coat. "She told him what she had done," said Max Palm III, Rose's grandson. "And that was the end of it." Max Palm, who lives in Finneytown, said that right after his grandmother died in 1929, his grandfather paid his first visit to the church.

"He was Lutheran," he explained.

The first Mr. Max Palm inspected the window, representing many things but among them his wife's mild insurrection. The inscription, in black Gothic lettering at the bottom of the window, reads "Presented by Mr. and Mrs. Max Palm in memory of Mr. and Mrs. John Bast."

So, Mrs. Palm used the mink money to finance a tribute to her parents and to shed beautifully colored light onto the heads of worshipers. There is no record of the exact amount of her donation, but archives note that several new stained-glass windows were installed at a cost of $12,000 to commemorate the Diamond Jubilee of the parish.

I like to think that upon reflection Mr. Palm believed that his wife had made a very fine decision.

The fur coat by then, surely would have gone wherever fur coats go when the moths are finished with them. And seventy-five years later, the window survives. The Palm window, entitled "The Finding of Jesus in the Temple," shows the Holy Family clustered to the right in the scene.

Jesus and Mary look serene. And Joseph looks a little worried.

This made me think of another nice Jewish family.

And another gift.

Mickey Kaplan, arts patron and wife of Dr. Stanley Kaplan, was approaching a "significant birthday, her seventieth. Her husband wanted to give her something special.

"I thought about jewelry," she said. Briefly.

Instead, she asked him to buy a new house. For somebody else. "One of those Habitat for Humanity houses like Jimmy Carter helps build," she said.

Habitat for Humanity helps low-income families buy affordable housing. Most of the work is done by volunteers, but they need money for materials and land. Then Habitat offers an interest-free mortgage, plus homeowners work a minimum of five hundred hours building the house. Mickey's house will have three bedrooms and one bath. It will cost her $45,000.

She could have had a very fancy necklace. Or, say, a fur coat. But like Mrs. Palm, she chose to do something more important, more lasting.

Max Palm died six years after his wife, and he never discussed the window with his children or with his grandson. So I suppose we will never know if, in the end, he was proud of the choice Mrs. Palm made.

But I have spoken with Stanley Kaplan, who said he thinks that his wife made a very fine decision.

—*March 1999*

35
Laura Pulfer

A Round Of Applause For The Sidelines

MOST OF THE WOMEN AT THE TABLE WERE FAMILIAR. Fellow breast cancer survivors, we've seen each other at benefits where you run for money or talk for money or eat for money. We've met at seminars and in hospital rooms and at memorial services.

My seat this time was next to a stranger, who introduced herself and said apologetically, "Uh, I'm not a survivor. I'm just a friend. I'm just here for her." In other words, she paid $35 for a plate of rubber chicken "just" to help cure a disease she didn't even have.

I thought of Ms. Just-A-Friend again when I read the news about the latest breakthrough in the treatment of cancer. Herceptin, which attacks the disease's genetic roots, is the result of two decades of cancer research. Thousands of lives will be saved. Or at least prolonged.

How many bike-a-thons and walk-aramas and wine tastings and fashion shows have collected money that wound up in the hands of scientists? How many men and women have volunteered to check coats and gather silent auction items? How many have offered up their bodies for research?

My own mother never missed an appointment with the doctors at the Barrett Center who were supervising the National Cancer Institute's tamoxifen study here. She drove her 74-year-old self two hundred fifty miles every time she was asked, not because she thought she might get cancer. But because she didn't want cancer to get my daughter.

Every year, thousands of people in Greater Cincinnati walk to raise money for multiple sclerosis. A motorcycle club dispatches members to intersections to guide walkers over the ten-mile course. High school kids sing and cheer at checkpoints along the way. Companies donate granola bars and pretzels and bananas and juice.

Men, women and children snake up through Mount Adams and around East Walnut Hills wearing T-shirts with things like "Willie's Walkers" and "Tom's Team" and "Mama's Hope" and "Michael's Angels."

A national survey on volunteerism found that most American adults—78 percent— serve as volunteers in some capacity. The study reports that people who would like to be doing more volunteer work are the ones who most feel the importance of what they're doing.

Makes sense.

The MS walk ends under a huge arch of balloons. As walkers finish, they pass a row of people in wheelchairs and on scooters, the "cheerleaders," who applauded each sweaty walker. Sometimes it was clear that the effort for them of bringing two hands together was more difficult, took more energy, than the preceding ten-mile walk for the rest of us.

But I can understand why the effort is made. They are grateful to those who have joined their personal battle. A thank-you is essential, for both emotional and practical reasons. Even if it's not easy.

Another cure on the horizon? Well, bravo to the doctors and scientists who battle cancer and cystic fibrosis and Parkinson's disease and muscular dystrophy and AIDS and multiple sclerosis. But let's not forget to give a great big roar of thanks to those who are neither medical experts nor sick, the people who are "just" friends.

Pat yourselves on the back, you runners and walkers and donors and guinea pigs. Give yourselves a big round of applause if you've licked envelopes and sat through interminable committee meetings.

Those of you who have held the hand of a spouse or a child or a friend or a neighbor, give yourself a cheer. Members of the casserole patrol—you tireless providers of food to the grieving, the weary, the sick—you are part of this, too.

This is your victory.

—*May 1998*

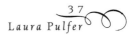

Tory Koch And Other Life Celebrations

A SEA OF FACES, MANY OF THEM WITH REDDENED EYES. Audible sniffling. Yet it was a celebration.

Patty Britton was speaking. Beautiful, articulate, a 31-year-old woman who needed—and got—a new liver. Voice a little unsteady, she thanked the people in the audience, families of those who donated organs, tissues and eyes last year.

More sniffling, dabbing at eyes. I noticed a man who simply let the tears roll down his cheeks and drip onto his jacket. I wondered whom he was remembering. I was remembering Victoria Koch. Tory. Age 14, owner of a purple bicycle, aspiring ballet dancer, saxophone player and thoroughly positive person.

Most of us heard about the little girl from Lebanon for the first time in February 1993, when she underwent a double lung transplant, radical treatment for cystic fibrosis. We followed her to the hospital many times, every one of those trips a new crisis for a child who probably never drew an unimpeded breath in her life.

Yet she smiled, on camera and off. An incandescent smile.

After her transplant, she said "I wake up, do the day, go to sleep, wake up, have fun. I don't think about death."

She played a page in a Cincinnati Ballet production of Cinderella, a cameo role. In real life, she was a star.

The Ohio Valley LifeCenter, which coordinates tissue and organ donations in the Tristate, had an unusually high number of donations in 1995, the year Tory died. The LifeCenter attributes the increase to Tory's public battle.

This year, donations restored sight to more than four hundred twenty-five people, rescued more than a thousand burn and accident victims who needed skin and bone grafts, and gave a second chance to one hundred twenty-two people who needed organ transplants.

"A few months before her death," a woman says, "my daughter and I went to get her a state identification card. My daughter was asked if she wanted to be an organ donor. She saw me cringe at the thought of death. Her exact words were, 'Maybe I could help someone see. Why wouldn't you want to do that?'"

Patti Britton was speaking at a celebration of lives saved and a remembrance of those who saved them. She fits into both categories.

Pregnant, she was hospitalized for what doctors thought might be a relatively minor problem. "Then something went terribly wrong," she says. "I woke up after being in a coma and was told I had a new liver." Her baby, Christopher, was delivered two months early, weighing only two pounds, and "we lost him four months later." Patty and her husband, Paul, became a donor family.

Three years have passed since their son's death. Patty and Paul have investigated adoption, and they're going to look into a surrogate program.

"We have so much love to share," she says. This is from someone who not only counsels transplant candidates but probably has baked and given away enough therapeutic banana bread and chocolate cookies to feed everyone in her neighborhood.

Obituaries often request memorials be made in the name of the person the family has lost. Because we don't want them to be forgotten. Ever.

And I just cannot imagine a finer memorial than giving more time on this earth to Tory Koch. Or a new life to Patty Britton—banana bread baker, doting wife, secretary, adoring daughter, support group leader—who dares to dream of being a mother again.

—*April 1998*

Door Creaks Open, Woman Slips Inside

A VERY POLITE, BUT EXASPERATED READER—a woman—wondered if I would write about bosses who don't harass their employees. "So many men are helpful to women in the workplace and at home. We never hear about them."

Well, of course this is not nearly as much fun as speculating about what transpired between the president of the United States and various paid and unpaid employees. But I promised her I would think about it.

So I did. And I'm thinking I know who these men are. I've worked for some of them. And sometimes they're strangers, somebody who reaches a door before me and wonders if he should open it. Step through? Wait? Will I think he is patronizing? Am I determined to be insulted?

Let me assure you, gentlemen of the world, I welcome your help. In fact, most women would not be offended by a sincere—or even insincere—hand with the dishes, with the sales reports, with an introduction to a potential client.

We wouldn't mind being included in your golf foursome if you're planning to discuss business. Or at the table at the Queen City Club if it will help us close a deal.

We are new to this. Our mothers stayed at home so our fathers, returning from the rat race, were not inconvenienced by dirty laundry, late meals or ill-mannered children. Some of our moms worked. But it was a job. They didn't run the show there either.

Now, some of us do. Not a lot. But some.

Karen Hendricks, for instance. She is chairman and CEO of Baldwin Piano & Organ Co. After twenty years at Procter & Gamble, she took over a division at Dial Corp. Then a headhunter approached her in 1994.

The venerable piano company had been hitting some sour notes. An inefficient Fifties-style manufacturing system, flagging sales, a stodgy image on Wall Street. It still had a great

name. Baldwin is the official piano of the Chicago, Philadelphia and Boston symphonies. Dave Brubeck and Billy Joel choose to play Baldwins.

But the company needed new life and a tough response to a changing world. Enter Ms. Hendricks.

She hired and fired. She cut costs. She divested. She reduced inventory and restructured financing with dealers. She beat back a stockholder challenge. She made friends with Wall Street. Income soared.

I mention these things only because Karen Hendricks has been asked to join the formerly all-male Cincinnati Business Committee.

Schools. Stadiums. Elections. These guys are always behind the scenes. With strategy. With money. With power. This makes the rest of us nervous because we like to reserve the right to mess up our own lives. But we have to admit that they are a very accomplished group of men. Overachievers, you might say.

I'd like to think they noticed female executives who have improved the fortunes of their companies. I hope they'd be embarrassed to belong to a group that refuses to admit women. But they were not required by law to do this. Nor were they trying to improve their resumes.

So, let's celebrate the appropriate entrance of this qualified woman to a powerful club. And let's not forget the men who opened the door.

—*March 1998*

Naked Truth About Life's Adventures

THERE ARE KIDS' TOYS AND NAKED PEOPLE all over the place. I'm standing in the middle of Leeanne Schmidt's house in Fort Thomas. Gaping. I hate to start with the most sensational part of what she does. But it is unavoidable.

On the living room and dining room walls, up the staircase and into the bedrooms are black-and-white photographs of elbows and hips and even more personal parts, all submerged or emerging from water. The bodies belong to young people and old people, men and women.

The toys belong to the artist's grandchildren.

It is all very wonderful, exotic and familiar at the same time. Those bodies don't belong to models, but they all are lovely nonetheless. Or at least interesting.

As is the artist, herself.

Leeanne Schmidt—a 58-year-old mother and grandmother, a former teacher, biochemist and hematologist—says she didn't know she was an artist until ten years ago.

Her new life began when one of her sons asked for a darkroom. So she read a book. Then she took a few photography classes. It became more than a passing interest, more like a passion. This is probably very baffling news to those of you out there who are younger than, say, 40. Or perhaps it is reassuring to know that this is not one of the things you will have to give up in later years.

It has been our little middle-age secret. Passion can strike at any age.

Leeanne got a scholarship to her alma mater. Then, exactly thirty years after her first degree from the University of Cincinnati, one in medical technology, she got another one. Her master of fine arts degree came in 1992.

She has been on an artistic roll ever since.

People pay up to $3,500 for her work, which hangs in more than one hundred fifty museums and galleries, including ones in New York and Paris and Denmark. She has traveled the country with a motorcycle gang. She has been a visiting artist in Columbus, Ohio, and Cairo, Egypt.

But lately and most successfully, she has been photographing nudes. And this from a woman who was "so shy as a child that when I went to the circus and the clown's pants fell off, I couldn't look."

Now she will go right up to complete strangers and "just ask them to take their clothes off, jump into a big bucket of warm water and let me photograph them."

Are you feeling as though you might like to go out for lunch and never come back? Maybe it's not your job. Or your family. Maybe you're just generally bored, thinking life has no more surprises to offer.

If this is the case, you may want to think about the woman who discovered she was an artist working as a medical technician. You might want to think about how she had the courage to open her middle-age eyes. It might help you to open your own.

—*December 1998*

4 2
Mothers and Other Heroes

Five

Amazing Grace And An Epidemic Of Goodness

Bonfield Girls Take A Last Walk

KRIS WESSELING'S SISTERS TOLD ME A WEST SIDE STORY. Oh, they didn't say so in as many words, but it had all the elements. Church. Family. A hint of politics. Honest sentiment. Even a bar famous for Irish wakes.

Kris was still in grade school when she learned she had diabetes, which would destroy her kidneys and shape her sisters' lives for the next forty years. During that time she went to college, got married and had a son. The last twenty years were a gift from modern medicine—and a sister.

Kristeen Bonfield Wesseling, who died in 1997, was Hamilton County's one hundred fiftieth kidney transplant patient. All three sisters lined up for antigen tests, hoping to be the one with the kidney least likely to be rejected. Karen Bonfield and Kimberly Bonfield Kemp matched. Kathy Bonfield Ruch didn't. After more elaborate profiling—weight, age, health, circumstance—Karen was chosen.

Lucky Karen.

Right after the operation, Kris was sitting up in bed, felling better than she had in years. Karen was on morphine. Kris had a relatively modest scar. The donor incision is huge, front to back in a half moon. A rib is removed.

"Well, I did feel lucky," Karen says. "We didn't know how much time this would give her, but I would have done it for any amount of time."

The Bonfield girls—these women—are the instantly likeable daughters of Maureen Bonfield, called "Mother" by hundreds of people who didn't actually grow up in her house. Some were patrons of the Crow's Nest in Price Hill.

After husband Charles—Kiestie—died in 1958 and Maureen sold the bar in 1972, she worked as a clerk-typist at Hamilton County Municipal Court, later as a bailiff and almost from the first day was "Mother" to judges and clerks and lawyers and reporters.

When the chips are down, you usually get the support group you've earned. And Maureen

Clark Bonfield and her family are entitled to every prayer said, every candle lit, every flower sent, every note written. They did it first and often. You might say it was genetic.

So, one sister gave Kris a kidney. Another one painted her fingernails. They called every day from Las Vegas when they took a vacation without her. Debbie Reynolds watched their luggage while they made the call.

They cooked and cleaned for Kris. They made her laugh. And they would gladly have done so for many more years. Gladly.

This is, I believe, the family values we hear about more often than we see.

When her sisters were asked to choose pall bearers to carry Kris's casket to the cemetery, they looked at each other and each knew what the others were thinking. Kathy said it.

"We carted her around in her wheelchair for nine years, we will carry her this last time." And they did.

—September 1997

Ruth Schmitt, An Epidemic Of Goodness

EVERY ONCE IN A WHILE—a great while—somebody comes along who is so thoroughly good that it is catching. Contagious, you might say.

When Ruth Schmitt was an insurance agent, for instance, she never forgot the person who sat down and wrote out a check for the premium. It wasn't a policy, she says. It was a promise. After she became a vice president, she trained the new agents to think the same way. When they got it right, I'll bet she rewarded them with a hug.

The Schmitt family is very big on hugging. Ruth's brother, Don, president and CEO of Shur-Good Biscuit Co., claims everybody needs at least seven hugs a day. He has an inexhaustible supply and throws in his choirboy smile for good measure. The smile falters just a little when he talks about his older sister.

Ruth Schmidt—business executive, golfer, poker player, godmother—has Alzheimer's disease.

It was shocking news for a family that calls Ruth "the clown, the adviser, the listener,

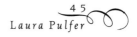

Laura Pulfer

the voice of reason." This is a woman who was always the donor, not the recipient. Scholarships and jobs for Seton girls. A place to stay for a temporarily homeless family.

Periodically, she'd swoop down on a blind couple in her neighborhood and off they'd go to the grocery in her big car. Her treat.

Her sister, Vivian Riestenberg, says she first noticed some things that were "very unRuthie-like." Some confusion with numbers. And dates. Diagnosed in 1993, Ruth continued for a while as usual. "But then," she says, "I just wasn't trusting myself anymore."

She tried to be practical. "You have to play the cards you're dealt," she says. But giving up her car two years ago was tough. Her automobile represented freedom.

Freedom, Aunt Ruth? You want freedom? You've got freedom, decided her twelve nieces and nephews. They rotated. A Ruthie week. They took her wherever she wanted to go, whenever she wanted to go there.

The plan was to give her the life she loved for as long as possible. So they put their own lives on hold. Just a little. The payoff, of course, was that if they were behind the wheel, the one in the passenger seat was Ruth Schmitt. Not a hardship.

"It was fun," Julie Hopkins says. "Very therapeutic." For the drivers, not the passenger.

This worked for about a year. But then Ruth needed more help. Around the house. Maybe, her family thought, it might be time for Ruth to leave her beloved condo.

Not yet, said her friends. Twenty-one of them made out a schedule of "sleep-overs with Ruth." These women—who began their friendship in grade school at St. Teresa Elementary School in Price Hill or at Seton High School or at endless poker games and parties—postponed the inevitable for ten months.

Then, Ruth moved out of her home into Bayley Place, a Delhi Township retirement community sponsored by the Sisters of Charity. Someone there told her gently that after the months of sleep-overs and tag-team help, "now your friends will become just friends again."

The day we met, she was going out to lunch with Vivian and Don. Neat, white tennis shoes, tailored khaki pants, magenta knit shirt, a careful touch of gold jewelry. Perfect makeup. Elegant.

She inclines her head with its halo of white curls and says, "I'm so glad we had this time

to talk." She clasps me in a hug. Just then, her blue eyes are clear and unclouded by confusion.

And for several priceless moments, I bask in the goodness that is Ruth Schmitt. Hoping to catch it.

—December 1997

Miz Ballew's Beauty Treatment

THE TABLE IS SET WITH BRIGHT YELLOW PLATES. The guest of honor walks down the hall with great dignity, leaning—but not too hard—on a cane. Her face is smooth, her hair jet black, except for a little patch at her right temple. She is due for a touch-up from her favorite hairdresser, Chawn the Ponytail Queen.

Miz Margueriet Ballew is 102 years old on this day. And I have come for her health and beauty tips.

An herbalist, Miz Ballew sometimes fills the air around her room at the Lincoln Center Nursing Home in Walnut Hills with the bracing aroma of spearmint. She makes hair conditioners and eye ointment. She collects vitamins. And ideas.

"Calcium," she tells me. "Take lots of calcium. Use vitamin E on your face. Drink lots of water."

"You have to keep busy." Well, that doesn't sound like much fun. I'd rather she prescribe something easier, say, a miracle drug.

She doesn't take any drugs. None? "Nope," says Mitzi Turner, activity director at the home. "She exercises, walks. And she stays active."

It's the habit of a lifetime.

Born in Richmond, Ky., Miz Ballew—not ms. or missus—lost her mother when she was 5. "I stayed with different people," she says. "And I tried to make myself useful."

She scrubbed floors, washed and ironed, pleated fancy curtains and made elaborate linens. Married young, she had two sons. "But I left my husband because he wanted to keep me pregnant all the time." She moved to Cincinnati and kept working, supporting her boys. "I had nobody to depend on but me."

 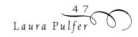

She sewed parachutes during World War II, operated the elevator at the old Gibson Hotel, sat behind a milling machine and lathe. She has catered and cleaned other people's houses. She has volunteered for the Red Cross and for politicians.

"I stuffed envelopes for Bob Taft."

The governor?

"Junie? No, for his daddy."

A lifetime of keeping busy.

"It's good for your circulation," she says firmly. "I used to be a good dancer. The two-step. Jitterbug. I used to love to go to the senior center on Wednesdays. More men." She looks at me carefully, so that I will get her meaning. I do.

While we're talking, a niece calls from Palm Beach to wish her a happy birthday. One son, who drove a bus in Cleveland, died years ago. She keeps in touch with her other son, who lives in California and has great-grandchildren and great-great grandchildren scattered all over the country.

She gets up from her chair, unassisted, and makes for the telephone. Her crepe-soled shoes creak a little, but not her bones. She wears a navy pantsuit with a knit shirt, two necklaces and an enamel and gold elephant pin. Pride.

She's no cardboard, little-old-lady saint. She sometimes leads the volunteers and employees on a merry chase to please her. She loves the spotlight, and, as one woman puts it, "She'll talk real smart to you." Sass. I like that.

Surely genetics is part of the mystery of Miz Ballew, who turned 102 with incredible verve. But there is something else, more than the herbs, the small meals of fruits and vegetables, the dandelion wine and vitamins.

"Think good thoughts," she says. "When somebody does something bad to you, don't get mad. Do something real nice for them. It will make you feel better.

"And it will drive them crazy."

—February 1999

Katy Conway Brings Out The Best In Us

CONSIDER THIS A thank-you note.

It's from the family of Cincinnati Police Officer Kathleen Shannon Conway. They cannot, they say, ever reach all the people who have sent flowers, written letters and cards and prayed for their Katy. And it is worth remembering that Officer Conway, praised by fellow officers for her bravery and professional composure, first was a "very special little girl."

She is Chris, Kevin and Michael's sister, Jacob's godmother, Jane's granddaughter, Tom's daughter. And very special indeed.

"Are you hurt?" asked the radio dispatcher, responding to a call for help from car 1212.

Officer Conway, covered in blood, shot four times, moments after returning fire with a gun she pulled from a holster on her fractured hip, replied, "That's affirmative."

That's affirmative?

Hell yes! would be more like it.

"Did you notice that there were no bad words on the tape?" says Katy's grandmother, Jane Keniston of Mount Lookout.

Well, to tell the truth, I hadn't noticed. But I noticed that this kid—and I mean no disrespect but she is only 23 years old—seemed uncommonly determined to survive. Faye Conway, Katy's mom, a first-grade teacher who lives in Anderson Township, shows me pictures from a family wedding. "Look at that red hair. Isn't that a sweet face."

I do. And it is.

And I know Faye Conway, who says Katy is bright and kind and "a very special little girl," has told her so. To her face. Many times.

When I went to University Hospital looking for the reason this young woman was so brave, I think I saw the answer right in front of me, wearing a black pantsuit and a weary smile. Pale blue eyes, gold wire-rimmed glasses pushed carelessly on top of her blond hair,

Laura Pulfer

this is one of those moms who lets her children know they are special and important.

It's not only something to live up to, but when the chips are down, maybe it helps them remember their lives have value.

Upstairs at the hospital, the solarium near Katy's room is clogged with people—family, police officers, friends. Some friends drove up from Louisville. "They knew they couldn't see Katy, but they came anyway," Mrs. Conway says. "Just to be here with us."

A couple of boys Katy met when she was "flipping burgers at Coney" raced to the hospital when they heard the news. "And they stood there while Katy was in surgery." Nearly three hours.

Police officers from all over the country have written. The ones around here have brought food. Strangers have offered Katy a puppy and a lucky penny and dinner.

A young girl wrote, "I got my ears pierced for my birthday. And I wasn't as brave as you."

Another letter came from a woman whose husband was arrested by Officer Conway for drunk driving. "You put your arm around me and said, 'It's gonna be all right,'" the woman wrote. "And it was." The woman said she would never forget the police officer's kindness.

Flowers, balloons, cards. People who want to shake her hand. People who want to take her to dinner. People who just want her to know that she is in their prayers.

And Katy? She is still a little confused and amazed that so many people know her story.

Well, Officer Kathleen Shannon Conway, we needed some good news. And a live hero. We have seen too many badges crossed with black tape.

We have been heartsick.

Faye Conway says she is grateful for the prayers and the "genuine concern." She knows her daughter "has a long recovery ahead, but we know she'll get better. She will heal."

Maybe we all will.

—*February 1998*

Paula Howard Tells The Secret Of Being Alive

I WISH I WERE GOOD ENOUGH—skilled enough—to make you feel what it was like in that room. Oh, it was just a hospital room. You know what they're like these days. Soft colors, faux wood, flowers, Mylar balloons, stuffed toys, cards.

The difference was the woman.

Her face, bright as a new penny, was topped by a brave nimbus of wispy light hair. Not nearly enough to cover her scalp, but it's all that survived a hundred chemotherapy treatments. Her eyebrows, another casualty, are penciled softly over deep blue eyes. She is wearing silky flowered pyjamas and a smile framed by carefully applied pink lipstick.

Paula Howard is celebrating. Unlike the wood, the celebration is not faux. This woman is sincerely, positively, amazingly happy. No wonder. Just when she was given a death sentence, she discovered life.

"My wife, Paula," dentist Bill Howard wrote in a letter to me, "was first diagnosed with breast cancer shortly before Christmas, 1989. Following surgery in January of 1990, the pathology report was ominous. All eight lymph nodes came back positive. We had about a year off before the first metastasis was detected on a bone scan in October of 1991."

"She has been in treatment ever since."

Ever since? My God. Where does that smile come from?

"I used to go through life as fast as I could, putting away dishes while I was talking on the phone," Paula says. "Rushing. Now I take note of everything. I listen, really listen to the sounds around me. See things. Feel things. I decided to make each day count. Every one."

She has traveled—Paris, Turkey. She saw her son graduate from college. "And I never thought I'd be lucky enough to see him through high school." Gardening. She always liked gardening. So, for the first time in her 50-plus years, she got competitive about it. She

51

Laura Pulfer

entered the Ault Park flower show two years ago. And won a blue ribbon and trophy.

Since 1991, she has been coming to University Hospital from her home in Clermont County every three or four weeks. The cancer is always there. The chemo doesn't cure it but suppresses it. She cannot go more than four weeks or it will rage out of control.

After her treatments, according to Bill, comes "hanging on through the following week to ten days of falling white cell counts, feeling tired and feverish, gastrointestinal upset and much more. Then, just as she is beginning to feel normal, it's time to go back to the hospital for another round."

He tells me this.

She tells me about spending Christmas in France and shopping for a wig. "I never have a bad hair day anymore," she says, laughing. The wig is for work in a department store. Her co-workers cover for her during the treatments. This life that she has claimed for herself is not a solitary achievement. She is buoyed by friends, her husband and their son, Trey. Her doctor, oncologist Elyse Lower, "walks on water."

Then, of course, there is faith. "I don't think God micromanages, but there is a bigger plan. Maybe God wanted a successful survivor, to give hope to others. I can honestly say that I have never been happier. There were times in my life when I felt buried alive. But not now."

Posted in her room is a quote from Marcel Proust: "The real voyage of discovery consists not in seeing new landscapes but in having new eyes."

I borrowed Paula Howard's eyes for just a moment, seeing a world of squandered time. And in that room, laughing with the woman sprawled across a starched expanse of hospital bed, it was easy to forget her struggle against death. Because she does so much living in between.

—*August 1998*

A Familiar Conspiracy Of Old Women

THEY CALL HER GRANMUDDY. It is, I assure you, a term of endearment.

Her name is Amanda McGhee, and she just turned 72. She is arthritic and diabetic,

bent a little by hard work. After she was widowed, sometimes she worked two or three jobs to provide for her three children. Hard jobs. Cleaning other people's houses, taking care of other people's kids. Sometimes she earned a little extra money by serving at parties.

You'd think she might want to just put her feet up and rest.

On the day we met, she was dressed for action. White tennis shoes, white socks and a plaid jumper. The action was her great-granddaughter, Kaela, not quite 2 years old. Bright, well-behaved but a handful.

Chasing her was not exactly what the doctor had ordered for her mother, Ingrid Jarmon-Thomas, recovering from a hysterectomy. And Ingrid, who teaches elementary school in Finneytown, had precious little time to recuperate before classes started.

So Granmuddy packed up her bags and came to help. As she always does.

There is, if you don't already know it, a conspiracy of women like Amanda McGhee. They head up the casserole patrol when somebody is sick or grieving. They know what to do for a baby with colic. They have sewing baskets and cookie sheets and aren't afraid to use them. They show up when they're needed.

They make things you can't buy. And they give time they don't have. If you're lucky like Ingrid and her husband, Ed, who works at Procter & Gamble Co., you're related to one.

If you're not, sometimes you can borrow.

Ms. McGhee, born in Knoxville, grew up in the West End then moved to Avondale. Her care packages go out to college students all over the country, filled with pecan sandy and tollhouse cookies. She dispenses homemade pound cakes and sweet potato pies to the old, the infirm and the lonely.

I don't mean to make her sound like a saint. For all I know, she sings off-key on Sunday mornings at New Prospect Baptist Church. Her pastor, the Rev. Damon Lynch III, says simply: "She is living out what we preach and teach. She is a care giver."

As we sit in the family's big beautiful house in Forest Park, she absently strokes Kaela's hair. I get the feeling she'd like to check on the laundry or iron something or bake something or mend something. Or something.

Someday, after I'm gone, I'm sure my granddaughter will say something like, "Boy, you just can't get cookies like Mamaw used to buy."

My homemade sugar cookies are like cuttlebone, and I mend hems with masking tape and staple guns. Small things. But will I come through for my little Rosie when she needs me for big things? Will I drop everything, put my life on hold if she asks? Will she ever think my story is worth telling?

Ingrid called me, she confesses, after Oprah turned her down. "So I called you, because I think people should know there are women out there like my grandmother. She is always doing things for other people. I don't know if this is the kind of thing newspapers print."

If it's not, it should be.

—August 1997

Six

Minor Miracles And Underage Role Models

TRAFFIC WAS BAD ON the interstate, so the two students from McNicholas High School, who call themselves "ordinary kids," took some side roads. They were on their way to the mall when they found themselves in the middle of a tragedy.

Matthew Trapp, 17, was driving, rounding a bend on East Broadway Avenue in Loveland. He saw a car stopped in the middle of the road, right behind a truck. As he pulled to the side of the road, his friend Amanda Miller, also 17, was already opening the car door.

"She basically hopped out of the car before I had it stopped," he says.

A little girl was lying by the side of the road. "I tried to get her attention by talking to her, touching her," Amanda says. Then the teen-ager put her face down to the little girl's mouth. "She wasn't breathing." Putting her fingers to the child's throat, the teen-ager found "a faint pulse."

This all took place in a matter of seconds. "A man kept telling me to leave her alone." She knew what he was thinking. Paralysis. "But she wasn't breathing. Her only chance to live was to get some air." So Amanda pressed her mouth over the child's, just as she had learned to do in her Red Cross lifesaving class.

"C'mon, baby, wake up," she heard a woman say in the background. Still, she continued, trying to breathe for Alesia Hill, 8, who fell into the path of a delivery truck. Amanda didn't give up until the paramedics arrived. The child was flown to Children's Hospital, where she was pronounced dead.

Whatever chance little Alesia Hill had for survival was because of Amanda, according to the Loveland police officer who investigated the accident.

Amanda and Matthew watched television news that Tuesday evening, just to confirm what they already knew. They have not tried to get in touch with the little girl's family, nor have they sought any further information.

"I don't feel like I need all the details," Amanda says.

Probably she has more detail already than most people could handle. She can picture "a sweet little face with pretty blue eyes," and when she closes her own eyes she still sees a partially eaten Hostess strawberry shortcake by the side of the road.

Twisting her hands a little, she says the obvious thing. "I wish I could have saved her." But she is qualified to say one other thing, something most of us ordinary people would like to be able to say in a variety of life circumstances—some as crucial as this one, some more trivial.

"I did everything I could."

—August 1999

If You're Sick Of Teen-agers, Try Irish Cure

THIS LITTLE MIRACLE CAME TOGETHER QUICKLY, but the most important part didn't happen overnight.

It begins with the immigration during the 1920s of the Magennis family from Northern Ireland to Brooklyn. Eight children, who couldn't get jobs because they were Catholic. And it ends at the very Catholic, very Irish McAuley High School in College Hill.

Sue Ward teaches social justice and spirituality to seniors there. This, I gather, is something like community service and religion and philosophy rolled into one, with a dab of history and a hint of sociology. But I could be making this up.

I am not making up the rest of it, although it sounds like an After-School Special. The good teacher. A death. A bunch of teen-age girls who perform an exceptional kindness. With nobody watching.

"I teach by telling stories, a lot of them about my family and growing up," Sue Ward says. A favorite aunt, Kathleen, figured large in her lessons. The second oldest of the Magennis children, Kathleen "had the whole Ellis Island experience."

And, later, the American experience. Good stories. Personal. And Mrs. Ward shared them with her classes. It was natural for her to ask her students to "pray for my little Auntie Kathleen" when she died Jan. 3 at age 99.

Laura Pulfer

"Mrs. Ward talked about her aunt nearly every day," says Annie Boh, a senior. The kids were surprised when their teacher said she wasn't going to the funeral.

One was bold enough to ask why. Money. Even with the bereavement rate, it was $400. "Not in the budget," Mrs. Ward said.

That was on a Monday. By the next day at 10 a.m., the girls had reserved a ticket and come up with money for the fare. It accumulated $2 and $3 at a time, with almost all the 223 students chipping in.

With uncommon foresight, they put together an envelope with enough money for a taxi from the airport and other essentials. Pizza and french fries were drawn on the outside. But this was only a suggestion.

They'd checked with McAuley's principal, Cheryl Sucher, to make sure Mrs. Ward could have the time off. "We didn't have to think twice," Mrs. Sucher says. "We took turns covering her class, of course."

Of course.

The plot involved many telephone conversations, a special talent of every teen-ager. "My big risk," the principal says, laughing, "was to give out the principal's home telephone number. I gave it to the ringleader and made her promise to swallow the slip of paper."

The ringleader, Annie Boh, has been caught doing this sort of thing before. Not too long ago, she discovered a classmate's family couldn't come up with the tuition for her senior year at McAuley.

So, Annie and her friends raised the money, thousands of dollars. But she does not want to talk about this. "It might embarrass somebody." The McAuley girls asked Mrs. Sucher to hand off the trip to their teacher for the same reason.

They enclosed a note:

"All your life, every day, you've given more than you will ever know. Now, it's your turn to take."

Is this story just a little too sweet for you? Well, then you may want to consider the sour side of it. Most school teachers can't automatically come up with hundreds of dollars for an unexpected expense, even though they perform one of the toughest and most important jobs in the world.

Not every kid goes to a school like McAuley. Not every teacher inspires this sort of behavior. "I just love them," Mrs. Ward says. "And I guess they love me back."

And, of course, this is the part that didn't happen overnight.

—January 1998

Crimes And Misdemeanours

NO BLOOD, NO SCANDAL, not even much of a crime. I'm afraid an account of trouble in this little park in Blue Ash will never make headlines.

Still, it seems like a story worth telling.

Brian Parsons, just turned 16, is working to become an Eagle Scout. This makes him special, but not unique. Dan Beard Council has about seventy thousand Boy Scouts. Of these, only about two percent will ever become Eagles, scouting's highest rank. They have to do considerably more than help little old ladies cross the street and tie square knots.

Joseph Fowler, a Loveland Eagle Scout, built a stone path at the historical society there this spring. Paul Sakalas, a McNicholas High School senior, fixed a trailer damaged by last year's floods. Williamstown, Ky., has freshly painted curbs thanks to Dewey Takacy. Eric Lafay gave his time to a shelter for cats.

Well, you get the idea.

Brian, a sophomore at St. Xavier High School, lives in Blue Ash and is a member of Montgomery Troop 674. He built swings for Hunt Park, at the corner of Hunt Road and Floral Avenue. Not kiddie swings, but substantial wooden bench swings. He thought they should be beautiful as well as useful.

Several generations live near this little rural oasis, surrounded by pretty Cape Cod houses and mulched flower beds. You are as likely to see somebody struggling with a walker as you are to see babies in strollers. A swing set, picnic tables, a bike rack. A little path. Trees and grass. Not fancy, but very peaceful.

It took nearly three months to complete Brian's plan. If this seems a little extreme for two simple wooden swings, it should be understood that Brian planned for these to last "forever." Or the teen-age approximation of that.

Every Saturday morning for seven weeks, he hammered and sawed and sanded. The benches were completed and installed on a Saturday. Brian's grandparents sat in the swings and had their pictures taken. That night, one of the swings was pulled from the frame. Vandals, perhaps. Brian thinks maybe he should have made them stronger. Test weight was 800 pounds. Anyway, they've been fixed. Stronger bolts.

Now, it's true somebody played too hard on Brian's beautiful redwood swings. Kids, probably. But nobody spray-painted them. And this young man's contribution to his community was taken seriously by the people in charge. "The city has been just wonderful," according to Brian.

He says he felt bad when he saw what had happened to the swings. But he's not worried. "The people in the neighborhood are very concerned about this park." He seems to think they'll take care of it.

Brian Parsons is not a saint or anything. Just a nice, hard-working person. Dependable. Possibly the tiniest bit naive and idealistic. Somebody might come back and test the strength of his swings, maybe even test the resolve of the city to keep them there. I'd hate to think so.

For now, I'd rather think about this nice kid, sanding a redwood bench on his Saturdays. Or another boy carefully designing a shelter for homeless cats.

It is worth remembering that teen-agers like these are special. But not unique.

—*May 1998*

It's Not The Hair,
It's The Head Underneath

I WON'T KEEP YOU IN SUSPENSE. The little girl wasn't hurt.

Only 6 years old, she was learning to ride her bike, on her way to the Madeira library, when she went careening out of control. She was headed for certain disaster when a teen-

age boy appeared out of nowhere and pulled her off her bicycle and out of the way of a van speeding toward her.

Just like in the movies.

The child was Katie Bauer. By the time the frightened little girl's tears were dried, the boy was nowhere to be seen. The family told everyone they saw about what happened, hoping somebody would know him.

He didn't stick around for thanks from Katie's mother because he was already late for dinner and was more interested in what his own mother would have to say about that. He was located through a school guidance counselor, who put the word out. The boy's sister realized it was him and gave him up.

Is that just like a sister, or what?

The hero is Matt Dunn, 13.

My favorite part of this story (besides that the little girl was unhurt, of course) is the way they identified Matt Dunn. They were looking for a boy with green-and-orange hair.

Matt told me his hair was not green and orange but blue and gold, Madeira school colors, and only because there was a pep rally that day. I was imagining the tantrum I would have thrown if my kid had come home with blue-and-gold hair, even for a pep rally.

And how wrong I would have been.

When Michael Snowden became Cincinnati's chief of police, he talked about another boy with, shall we say, interesting hair. He electrified the audience at his swearing-in ceremony when he talked about his son, Michael Jr., who played in a rock band and whose bright red hair fell in waves past his shoulders.

Young Michael wasn't there to see his father become Cincinnati's top cop. In 1991, when he was just 20 and just starting his second quarter at UC, a car driven by his fiancee slammed into a tractor-trailer on a Sunday afternoon.

His father said the young man's death was "the hardest thing I've ever had to deal with" and that Michael taught him "to learn to not prejudge people."

Michael, according to his father, "looked like a dope addict," which couldn't have been further from the truth. "I learned so much from him in his short life," Snowden said at the ceremony.

Today, the chief says that his son "changed me personally and the way I deal with the whole issue of prejudice. I really do try not to look so much at the differences, but at the things that are the same."

As a member of a generation that spent most of the 1960s fighting with our parents about our hair—we even had a play about it—you'd think people our age would know better. And yet, I can remember many bitter disputes with my own child about her hair.

Meanwhile, I liked everything else about her. Why on earth did I spend so much time nagging her about her hair? The color. The length. The style.

"We are all asking ourselves what is going on with the kids where 8-year-olds are killing one another and have no respect for human life," Katie Bauer's grandfather wrote to a Madeira city official. "Maybe we have a chance here to show the kids of our area that it is worthwhile to get involved, to respect human life and help out those that need it."

And maybe they have something to teach us.

Michael Snowden and his wife had this engraved on their son's tombstone:

"Accept me for what I am, not for what you think I am."

Katie Bauer's grandfather said, "We do have kids out there that do care."

And they might have long, red wavy hair. Or a mohawk. Or dreadlocks. Or it might even be blue and gold.

—December 1995

A L e s s o n F r o m T h e B i g G u y

THE CHILD, CLEARLY WORRIED, glances up at the clock again, light glinting off his round, wire-rimmed glasses.

"He's late," the little boy says to no one in particular.

The children in the classroom are very busy—engaged, you might say. They are making their computers beep. Some are studying the old-fashioned way, reading, writing in journals, drawing. There's an occasional outbreak of giggles.

Joy, apparently, is permitted.

No matter what they are doing, the kids have at least half an eye on the door. They are waiting for Steve. He is usually on time.

"It's him," shouts a little girl in faded jeans.

A slight young man ducks his head into the room. A cheer erupts. He is surrounded briefly, then he peels a boy from the group and goes out to the hallway.

Steve Bybee, a Harrison High School senior, is a tutor at Harrison Elementary. He's taking proficiency tests this week, which robs him of twenty minutes with the kids. So, he gets right to it, reading a bit, prodding gently.

He takes this job seriously, is absolutely faithful about showing up every day. Even though he is not paid to do it. Even though it costs him a study hall he could probably use. Even though he doesn't plan to be a teacher.

Originally, he was supposed to work with kids having trouble reading. But then, "everybody wanted to spend time with him, so he reads with all of them," teacher Joann Bernecker said. Sometimes the kids need something else. He supplies that, too.

"If somebody is having a bad day, I don't have to say much to him," Joann says. "Maybe just a wink or something, and he knows what to do." Maybe he'll put the book aside and pick up a basketball.

Joann trusts Steve to know.

One little boy runs a hand through his dark hair, struggling. But succeeding. "At the beginning of the year, I was worried about him," Steve says later. "But just the week before Christmas, there was a dramatic change."

The boy's mother thinks Steve is the reason.

This handsome boy—who is at the top of his class scholastically, who plays two varsity sports, who is an officer in every school organization he belongs to—thought of extra ways to help this child, tried to make him feel special.

And didn't give up.

"He's a role model for a lot of these kids," Joann says.

I paw through a stack of papers written by the kids. Steve has taught them Spanish. Steve has made Rice Krispie treats for them. Steve made them feel better when they were sad. Steve helped them make ornaments for their Christmas trees. Steve helped them find their way on the Internet.

Laura Pulfer

Steve. Steve. Steve.

A week ago, the school principal wrote a note to parents explaining some building maintenance, and asked teachers to send it home with their students. "Be sure to take it home," Joann warned, joking, "because it's from The Big Guy."

They all assumed she meant Steve.

The next time you wonder about the future of this country, picture a young man with his legs scrunched underneath a little table, reading to a child. Remember this 18-year-old who "worries" about a little boy struggling with schoolwork and a fractured family.

A role model? Of course he is.

But not just for second-graders.

—February 1999

F i f t e e n   M i n u t e s   O f   F a m e

PLEASE UNDERSTAND THAT I already know this isn't fair, but I'm going to do it anyway.

Two Anderson Township teen-agers found $10,000 in a trash bin and did not steal it. This extraordinary event made its way to the front page of *The Enquirer,* at least three radio stations and, eventually, onto national television. No less than Good Morning, America interviewed Matt Disher, 14, and Kris Miller, 15.

Here's what happened. Matt pitched his Spree candy wrapper toward a trash bin next to an ATM machine. It missed, and when he bent down to retrieve it and try again, he saw bundles of cash. Now, right away, I love the idea that he was persistent about using the trash bin.

Next, the boys checked to see if it was real. They then replaced the money and called police five hours later. During that time, they said they talked about a drum set that Matt wants and some car speakers Kris covets.

I think it was probably like the period of time between when I buy my lottery ticket and when someone else wins.

Eventually, they turned in the money.

They are not heroes. They are nice boys who did the right thing—after, it would appear to me, wrestling with their conscience, a drum set and some car speakers. Hey, I'm not making any judgements. I fear that I might still be wrestling. And losing.

About a week later, two other boys, exactly the same age as Matt and Kris, chased a robbery suspect and held him until police arrived.

Justin Evegan, 14, and Donte Ulmer, 15, both of Walnut Hills, had missed their downtown bus to school when a man grabbed a woman's purse. The woman, Carolyn Johnson, was in a wheelchair outside the John Weld Peck Federal Building when a man grabbed her wallet from the purse around her neck.

Then, "he just ran smack in front of us," Justin said. "Me and Donte heard the lady saying, 'Get him, get him,' and we just jumped up and took off after him."

That's my favorite part. It was instinctive. They didn't have time to think it over. On top of that, when they caught the guy, he threw some of the money at the boys. "He was like, 'Here, take some of the money and let me go,'" Justin said.

No dice.

They held him until police arrived. "When your brain clicks, you just do it," Justin said.

Maybe it is what we do without thinking that is truly heroic. I've never been tested, but I've always hoped that I would automatically do the brave and honorable thing.

So, as I said, it's really not fair to compare the two incidents, assigning a greater value to reflex. Maybe it's simply good news and better news. I'm not sorry that the two kids from Anderson got so much attention.

But, Donte and Justin, I hope you get your fifteen minutes of fame and more. I hope your family and friends and radio and television fawn all over you. And I have only one more thing to say: I want to be just like you when I grow up.

—*March 1996*

Seven

Just Because They Don't Blab You Secrets Doesn't Mean They're Dumb

Measuring His Kindness By The Pound

FIRST OF ALL, LET ME SAY THAT I am not one of those who thinks animals are more important than people. It just turns out that I like almost every animal I meet. Especially horses. Inevitably dogs.

The SPCA, the animal shelter, the pound, is a dangerous place for me to be. When I walk down that aisle between the cages of dogs available for adoption, I want to save them all. Except for the big, mean-looking ones. Then I want someone else to save them.

But I do want them to be saved.

Pippin comes to the chain-link fence to look me over. Somehow, he can tell I am not a serious customer, and he retires to his corner. Tan and white, he's an improbable mix of boxer and terrier. Distinctive, you might say. A sign on his cage says he's housebroken and "good with people." He was given up, a note says, because he "needed a better home."

Often, the reason cited for bringing animals to the shelter is that the owners are moving and pets aren't allowed in their new place. One note says, "wife no longer wants to care for dog." So, what's wrong with you, buddy? Maybe it's your turn.

Most of the notes say simply, "stray."

My tour guide is Harold Dates, who stops to pet the dogs and the cats as we pass. He can't help himself. He likes them. And he wants them saved too.

Mr. Dates, who has a degree in sociology from the University of Cincinnati, wisely decided that animals were more interesting than people and went to work for the Society for the Prevention of Cruelty to Animals twenty-one years ago. In 1986, he became general manager. At the time, there was no spay-neuter clinic and no veterinarian on staff. Besides fixing both those things, he organized a network of local vets who are available to the SPCA twenty-four hours a day, seven days a week.

In 1975, the SPCA here "dealt with" more than thirty-six thousand animals. That number is down to around twenty thousand. Lots of adoptions, some lost pets claimed, some destroyed. Fewer every year. The spay-neuter clinic, Mr. Dates says, substantially reduces the number of strays.

Nationally, Mr. Dates is known as the organizer of disaster relief for animals, especially during floods. Three years ago, he started the equivalent of a soup kitchen for dogs and cats. "A lot of people were bringing in pets and saying they couldn't afford to feed them. His golden retriever, Sol, is a therapy dog who visits the sick, so Mr. Dates has seen firsthand that pets can be just what the doctor ordered.

And maybe if you don't have very much, a good dog is exactly what you need. A dog thinks you're a huge success even if your boss doesn't. And he'll give you a warm welcome if you live alone, plus plenty of reasons to get fresh air and exercise. For that reason, Mr. Dates has arranged for people 60 or older to get a free cat or dog and free instructions. They meet every Thursday. If you ask me, by now, their pets are as trained as they are every going to be. It's just an excuse to get together and check up on each other.

Harold Dates doesn't care.

Look, I am not saying he's perfect. For all I know, he eats ice cream directly from the carton. But, from everything I see and hear, this is a very good guy to have on your side. Like Pippin, he's kind of an improbable mix. He's part smart administrator, part softie. A formidable fund-raiser, he just can't wait to give it away. Distinctive, you might say. "Good with people," too.

His business is saving creatures. Unconditional love, I believe they call it. In other words, Harold Dates doesn't count feet before he decides whether to help.

—*January 1997*

The Dog Days Of The Bankers In Northside

EVERYBODY IN NORTHSIDE WHO KNEW THEM sensed something was wrong when they saw Bruce Heaton without his dog, Butch. And there was.

Somebody had lured the stocky little Boston terrier into a car and raced off. One of the neighbors saw it happen, but couldn't catch the guy. After a while it became clear that Butch was gone for good.

"If he was alive, he would have come back to Bruce," says his friend, Marcia Chadwick, a teller at North Side Bank and Trust Co.

It seems particularly cruel.

Bruce Heaton can't exactly go right out and find another pet. He needs a special dog. Bruce, 39, can't hear very well and is losing his sight. Two older sisters and one brother have died of the degenerative muscle disease that put him in a wheelchair.

Over nine years' time, the man and his little dog had kind of adjusted to each other. As Bruce's condition worsened, Butch picked up some of the slack. Once when the man fell out of his chair, the little black-and-white dog ran to a neighbor's house and barked until she followed him.

Just like Lassie.

And, of course, Bruce took care of his dog. Sometimes it was the only reason he got out of bed in the morning, certainly the only reason to pull himself into his chair and go outside.

It was a shame, everybody agreed. Janet Williamson, who's head of personnel at the bank, said "a bunch of us here decided we'd try to find a new dog for Bruce." They were thinking maybe one of those service dogs could help him with a few things around the house.

Scott Morgan, auditor at the bank, found out that these dogs cost in the neighborhood of $2,000. At least.

Then he saw a story in *The Cincinnati Enquirer* about a prison training program, and it

gave him an idea. He called the man in charge of the Rover Rehab program at Warren Correctional Institution, where dogs are rescued from the pound and trained by inmates.

Scott explained the circumstances to prison officials. They have only fifteen dogs in the program, but Scott is a pretty good explainer.

And one of the inmate-trainers began to prepare Billy to become Bruce's new best friend. A purebred Dalmatian about a year old, the dog is being outfitted with a special harness, equipped with saddlebags, so he can help pull Bruce's wheelchair.

Angel Griffis, the bank's receptionist, along with Scott, Marcia and Janet took Bruce to the prison to meet Billy. Nobody remembered to bring dog treats, so somebody gave Bruce a bag of people snacks. He sat there, smiling, his fingers orange with Cheeto dust.

"This dog is perfect," Bruce said.

Billy can pick up objects dropped to the floor and is learning to operate light switches and open doors. But he already knows how to be a dog, which is the most important thing. You know, wagging tail, sloppy kisses, not asking any dumb questions, acting as though the world revolves around you. These are incomparable services, as any dog owner will tell you.

For Bruce, they are a reason to get up in the morning.

—November 1998

An Alley Cat's Holy Rescue Squad

THE CAT IS NAMED VINCENT VAN GOGH because of his ears. The vet says he'll probably lose them.

Frostbite.

Vincent—Vinnie to his friends—used to prowl an alley in Over-the-Rhine with a bunch of other cats. They were starving, skinny, sickly, wild. Toni Cashnelli, who works for the Franciscan Friars on Vine Street, started catching them.

"I figured I could at least take them to a vet, have them neutered and spayed." A worthy goal, considering that one cat and her unaltered offspring could produce four hundred twenty thousand more cats in seven years.

After they were doctored and fed, Toni planned to let them loose again, maybe a little better able to fend for themselves. She's been reading a lot about feral cats. Vinnie must not have read the same books. Or, more probably, he was never wild.

He doesn't look wild. Bony still, he asks politely to be petted. Toni scratches his head, careful of his ragged ears. The tips, which have been frozen, probably will drop off eventually.

He flops on his side, then rolls over to have his stomach rubbed. "He has a wonderful nose, don't you think?" Toni says. It looks ordinary to me, pinkish and broad. She calls it leonine. I think comparing this poor little waif to a lion is a stretch.

But Toni would like to find a home for him. She can't put him back out on the streets. Although he's only about a year old, he will surely die. For one thing, she believes he was a house cat. "Does he look wild?"

Well, no, he doesn't. He walks over and trains his yellow eyes on me. Blinks once. Twice. Then, with great dignity, gently rubs against my outstretched fingers. Maybe that nose is a little leonine, now that I see it up close. And I am picturing the way he must have looked when somebody first got him, a little gray-striped ball of fluff.

Then maybe he got gangly and started acting like an adolescent, and somebody just tossed him out. "Like garbage," Toni says indignantly. He had no more idea of how to forage for his own food or protect himself against the real wild cats than any of the rest of us would if we'd been thrown suddenly on the street. In an alley.

Worse, he was bitten or scratched by a cat with feline immunodeficiency virus (FIV), the equivalent of AIDS for cats.

So Toni Cashnelli is dreaming, in my opinion. She is hoping that somebody out there would be willing to adopt an undistinguished alley cat (notwithstanding his aristocratic nose) who is missing his ears and is living with a death sentence.

"You can't catch FIV from a cat," she says. Nor can a dog or horse or gerbil or any other animal besides a cat. The only way it spreads is through blood—bites or transfusions. Prognosis is uncertain. With proper care, an infected cat could live a year. Or ten years.

"Vinnie could live a long, happy life," Toni says. "He just wants to be in somebody's home. Being loved."

Dreaming. She's dreaming.

Or maybe it's faith. She would certainly be in the right place for that, the Province of St. John the Baptist, a holy fixture of Over-the-Rhine since 1844. Friars from this beautiful old building at Vine and Liberty streets went on to Louisville, Detroit and New Orleans. Missionaries traveled to New Mexico, Arizona and China. They leave this serene place to help with hospices, schools, hospitals. They serve the homeless, the hungry and people with AIDS.

The Franciscan Friars, of course, were founded by St. Francis of Assisi. Their mission includes "reverence for every creature." And I hope the nice men I met at the province won't think me irreverent when I say that they remind me of a cheery, brown-robed rescue squad, poised to help anybody who needs them.

Even a sick little cat.

—April 1998

A Yelp For Help

OUR DOG MURRAY IS WORRIED. He even seems a little depressed. He has not said so in as many words—and, of course, I would be shocked if he did—but I think he is afraid he has been wasting his time on us.

Murray Kempton Pulfer has spent the last two years of his life training me and my husband, and he suspects that we are going to throw it all away on drugs. A collie, from a very distinguished family, Murray undertook our education immediately upon his arrival at our home.

He whizzed on the floor.

This was our first lesson. Since then, we have learned that while he would prefer to use the outdoor facilities, he is not a fanatic. We must open the door for him. He is not going to risk damaging his personal kidneys by prancing around "holding it" until we get around to letting him out. Besides, it's not dignified.

During the first few months after he came to live with us, in addition to his puppy chow, he ate a tube of Neosporin, a pound of bananas, a chocolate layer cake, a sock, three Reeboks,

two library books, a window sill and the leg of my favorite wing chair. We thought he might outgrow this. And he did.

He started eating bigger things, beginning with a couch.

This was his signal to us that he was bored. And lonely. We gave him big meaty bones and expensive chew toys. We bought a bigger car, so that he would be comfortable on long trips. And short ones. We started going more places together.

This was in the old-fashioned days before we heard about Clomicalm, which the Food and Drug Administration has approved to treat doggy "separation anxiety."

A man named Moussaieff Masson, a "psychoanalyst and student of animal emotions," told a CNN audience that the new drug should not be used because "there is no consent from the dog."

He said this with a straight face.

"I'd be glad to see a magic pill," said Dr. Tamara Goforth, the vet for the SPCA here, "but I don't believe anything is that easy. Even the manufacturer says it should be used in conjunction with training." And you have to remember, Dr. Goforth says, sometimes dogs just do doggy things.

Thank goodness.

Dog are much nicer than most people. They are more forgiving, more generous and certainly less inclined to talk behind your back. They do not fear commitment, nor do they demand expensive jewelry.

Do we really want to make them just like us? Their dogginess is the reason we like them so much in the first place. Worse, do we want to drug them into submission?

Murray hasn't said so, but I think his opinion would be that those people who want their dogs to smell like spearmint and who are willing to give them a pill instead of a good romp in the park probably are not really looking for a dog at all. I think he would suggest that you might want to just go out and get yourself a nice Beanie Baby.

—*January 1999*

Last Chapter In Dramatic Horse Rescue

A VILLAIN, A BUNCH OF GOOD GUYS, a kid and a yearling horse that nearly died. This is a pretty good story.

On a chilly winter day, the Highland County Humane Society went to a Hillsboro farm and started rescuing horses. Arabians with fancy bloodlines, they were starving. Some had to be carried. Two died, leaving one hundred sixteen very needy horses.

Their owner, Bill Sheets, was found guilty of ten counts of cruelty to animals.

Meanwhile, a bunch of do-gooders—and I say this with near reverence—took on the care of the survivors. FFA kids built feed troughs. Volunteers helped groom and nurse them back to health. There were mares, some with babies, and stallions in every Arabian color, mostly bays and chestnuts with a sprinkling of grays and blacks.

There were no geldings. "Sheets didn't believe in gelding," says one of the volunteers. "He thought it was inhumane. He didn't mind starving them." Mention the name Sheets around Hillsboro, and everybody knows who he is. He is the villain.

Now, I would like to introduce you to some of the good guys. Luanna Fairley took in eighty-three of the horses and tended them on her three hundred fifty-acre farm. Her daughter, Wendy, 9, fell in love with a scrawny little black and gray yearling filly. Her growth is stunted from malnutrition, and she wheezes a little when she runs. But she followed Wendy around like a dog. The child called her Kandy.

Most of the other horses have names like Zairafan or Xilpah, whose sire was named El Reata Juan, which made her worth $9,000 to a breeder.

The Highland County Humane Society got permission to auction the horses seized from the farm, and word got around, bringing buyers from eight states. Some were like a woman from Vermont, who drove all night with her daughter "to save a horse." Every last horse was sold, including three or four one-eyed horses and a few that were lame.

There were a couple of the dreaded "horse killers," who'll pay about eighty cents a pound for dog food or to sell abroad as people food. But most of the fifteen hundred people crowded into the Union Stockyards on Friday night were horse lovers who cheerfully outbid the butchers.

Sitting along one side of the auction ring wearing a red jacket and a worried expression was Patti Wooton of Felicity. There was only one horse she wanted. "I didn't know anything about this horse's lineage," she says. "Something just came over me. She's just the sweetest little thing. Her mother died at birth, and I know she just needs a lot of love."

Her growth is stunted from starvation, and she wheezes a little when she runs. Patti called her Destiny.

At 11:45 that night, No. 113 was led into the ring. Depending on your point of view, she was Destiny or Kandy. She'd been appraised at $125.

Auctioneer Lyle Flach looked at the child with the heart-shaped face in the front row. "Well, Wendy," he said. "Where do you want to start the bidding?" She started at $200. In less than two minutes, the bidding was up to $4,000. There were only two bidders. Wendy dropped out. She threw herself into her father's arms and sobbed.

"At midnight, I was standing there paying for my horse," Patti says. "People were glaring at me. I felt like a penny with change coming back. I bawled like a baby coming home, but I think this little horse was put on this Earth for me."

The sale grossed $155,450. That won't pay all the bills, according to Anne Tieman at the humane society, but "it's two or three times what we thought we'd get."

Destiny is on a twenty-five-acre farm with a woman who's determined to give her the best possible care. Wendy, a nice kid, mopes a little. The money she saved to buy Kandy is still in her college fund.

As I said, it's a pretty good story, but I would change the ending if I could.

—*October 1995*

Working Like A Dog

THE FIRST TIME I SAW A DOG IN A HOSPITAL was at Drake, where I was visiting a boy paralyzed in a diving accident. A nondescript black dog sashayed into the room and clambered quietly onto his bed. I looked around for the germ police, but nobody was paying any attention.

The dog waited a few minutes, then slipped her nose under the boy's hand. The boy could not move anything but his eyes. The dog wriggled a little closer, until the boy's limp hand rested firmly on her head. He grinned as he watched his hand doing the first normal thing since the accident.

It must have taken a person a long time to teach a dog this excruciatingly careful bedside manner. But that was another dog, another time.

This story is about Keeper, who visits Hospice every Wednesday, roaming from room to room on a red leash, paying calls on the residents of this hospital for the terminally ill. On the other end of the leash is Keeper's keeper, Betsy Stadnik. As usually is the case with completely wonderful dogs, this one has no pedigree and was a stray.

Black with brown eyebrows, Keeper most likely is a Labrador-Doberman mix. She's calm and friendly, but she has attitude. On this day, she seems distracted, perhaps missing one of her favorite patients, Tom Marrs, who died last month.

According to a rather adoring volunteer staff, Keeper was one huge, regular bright spot in the man's life. His family, in fact, insisted that the dog be allowed to come to the funeral. Which she did. She was accompanied by her owner.

Betsy Stadnik, a nurse, took Keeper to classes to qualify as an official therapy dog, and is chauffeur and sidekick. Betsy and Keeper are two of about three hundred fifty Hospice volunteers who tend patients, do various scut work or raise money. The fact is, this city would grind to a charitable halt without people who donate their time.

They are all over the place, and I challenge you not to know one. Boy Scout leaders, room mothers, teacher's aides, cookie bakers, fund-raisers.

Laura Pulfer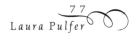

Anyway, Keeper is a therapy dog for Hospice, visiting the gravely ill, going from room to room in her red collar with the official tag and volunteer ID. But Keeper is, after all, a dog. She doesn't have a bus pass. So Betsy Stadnik takes her there. Every Wednesday without fail.

The best human interest stories, really, are still the ones starring humans.

—April 1996

Racing To Save The Losers

AT FIRST, YOU COULDN'T SEE WHAT WAS going on. The television camera caught jockey Chris Antley wallowing in the dust at the finish line at Belmont Park. An inglorious spill? He struggled awkwardly to his feet, still clutching the horse's reins. Then he cupped the big colt's left front foot in his hand.

Charismatic's rider, as it turns out, was making an entirely glorious rescue.

Doctors say Chris Antley probably saved the chestnut thoroughbred's life, preventing the horse from putting weight on the shattered bones in his leg. As the winner of the Kentucky Derby and Preakness was loaded onto an ambulance, cameras again zoomed in on his rider. Close enough to record the tears streaking his dusty face.

Critics say trainer D. Wayne Lukas pushes his horses too hard. It happens. And not just to horses. Some furiously competitive soccer daddies forget the combatants are 9-year-old girls. And some gymnastics coaches demand punishing feats, performed on delicate knees and still-growing tiny ankles.

Human athletes can be patched up and go on to other things, choose another line of work. Dot Morgan offers the same chance to racehorses.

Director of the Ohio Harness Horsemen's Association and a successful trainer, she runs a rescue program. Charismatic, of course, won't need her services. He is in a cast, four screws embedded in his very valuable left front leg. If things go well, his life will be an endless round of lush grass, classy lodging and ready mares.

But most retired racehorses aren't so lucky. A lot of them have injuries that will take a

while—an expensive while—to heal. Some are gelded. Others just don't know how to do anything but run around a track. Many are sold for slaughter.

Dot Morgan's files, she says, are full of people who want horses. "The hearts of people out there are big," she says. "I am just standing in the gap for horses until we can match them up."

She retrains them, then puts them up for adoption. An equine specialist who graduated from the University of Kentucky, Dot thinks of it as simply teaching the horse a new skill, "like sending a kid to vocational school. During the past seven years, more than three hundred horses have been shipped for rest and rehabilitation to Dot at her farm just northwest of Dayton, Ohio. This year, she expects to rescue between seventy and eighty horses, both thoroughbreds and trotters.

Some owners and trainers see these beautiful animals as trophies. Or as a big four-legged chunk of cash. Or as an indisputable symbol of wealth and status. You can buy a fake Rolex, but racing horses take real money. The sport of kings.

"But I also know owners who live in a tack room because that's all they can afford," she says. "Then something happens to their horse and instead of getting the $500 or $600 they could get from a trader, they'll give the horse to me, ask me to find it a good home."

So if you think Chris Antley was crying because he just lost the Triple Crown, then you don't know very much about horses.

Or the people who rescue them.

—*June 1999*

Eminent MD Paid Peanuts For Housecall

THEY ARE A NICE LITTLE FAMILY. Cute baby. Protective dad. Well, he's the step-father really. The baby's biological father lives in Philadelphia, and although the parting was amicable, he has started a new life and had little interest in the mother or their son.

Then the young mother developed a lump on her breast.

Dr. Donna Stahl didn't object when the step-dad insisted on peering over her shoulder during the examination. Although, to tell the truth, she thought he was a little scary. He's very hairy and weighs 500 pounds.

The patient is Kweli, a gorilla. At first the lump was about the size of an egg. Cancer? Infection? A benign tumor? Mark Campbell got on the Internet, looking for information about gorillas and breast disease.

Nothing.

Then somebody told him about Donna Stahl. Probably the best-known local expert in diseases of the human breast, Dr. Stahl has a soft voice and a completely kind face. Gentle hands. Animals apparently value these qualities as much as we humans do.

Kweli placidly slurped Gatorade while the physician palpated her breast. No tranquilizers. No drugs. Nothing that might harm the baby, Kicho, who is still nursing. Meanwhile, Colossus jealously oversaw the whole procedure from his adjacent cage. He is the long-time zoo resident probably most famous for what he does not do. Which is make babies of his own.

Chaka, a 14-year-old silverback, on loan to our zoo, is Kicho's father. Back now in Philadelphia after five years here, Chaka left behind eight babies and "a lovely parting gift," according to the zoo's general curator Mike Dulaney. Rosie, a 25-year-old western lowland gorilla, is expecting.

Colossus still has not selected a mate. "Performance anxiety," is Mr. Dulaney's opinion. Plus is in his 40s, elderly by gorilla standards. Maybe, I suggest, they could tell him about Warren Beatty. Dr. Campbell is still hoping Colossus might "interact," as he delicately puts it, with his female neighbors. "He is in excellent condition."

So is Kweli. As it turned out, her problem was a blocked milk duct. She's back to normal, but Dr. Campbell will add Dr. Stahl's name to his list of consulting physicians, along with cardiologists and ophthalmologists and dentists and gynecologists who normally treat humans.

"I think they do it because they are curious. And they know it's important. We are in this together."

Not just Kweli and Colossus. Not just doctors and vets. Everybody. Dr. Campbell has just returned from a trip to South America to help reintroduce macaws to their natural habitat, "trying to repair broken strands of the web," he says. "There's a reason things were put on this earth. A reason. We are interrelated."

One endangered species leads to another. And another.

Once you believe that, it's probably not much of a stretch to ask an eminent physician to put her hands through the bars of a cage to treat a sick gorilla, an ailing member of an endangered species. Mark Campbell says it is our obligation to take care of each other.

It's not just nice. It's the only way to live.

—August 1999

Eight

Behind Every Good Idea Is The Good
Person Who Dreamed It Up

Send Your Specs On An Overseas Trip

THE FIVE MOST ANNOYING WORDS in our house are: Have you seen my glasses?

They could be anywhere. In my husband's case, they probably are under a table at a restaurant. He needs them only to read menus. I don't have to wear my glasses all the time either—just when I want to see. So I don't wear them in public. I wear them when I'm reading in bed or watching Ally McBeal or checking my e-mail. The rest of the time, I squint or wear contact lenses.

After my last eye exam, I was told I might have to wear my glasses more often. In public. So I bought a new pair, which make me look just like Cameron Diaz—if Cameron were older, fatter, not at all beautiful and had a dimple-ectomy. (If we're ever invited to the same party, we'll probably have to wear name tags to avoid confusion.)

I hate to throw away my old glasses. They were expensive and have served me well. So as a going-away present, I'm giving them a trip abroad. LensCrafters and Lions Clubs International will take them on their next "mission," aboard a plane bound for a developing country.

They call it the Gift of Sight (GOS). Since 1991, twenty-six missions to seventeen countries have delivered free eye exams and recycled glasses to 313,458 people. It's not "cause-related marketing," the latest buzzword to describe a program in which you use your credit card and, say, a penny goes to research. Or maybe you buy a car and the dealer donates some of the money to a good cause.

This one is pure philanthropy. Unless you count what happens to a company where employees use their break time to wash, sort and repair old eyewear. Or what happens when departments begin to form teams to see who can put together the most packages to go overseas.

And, of course, you can't really calculate what happens to an employee who actually sees "the magic moment." That's what they call it when a person can see for the first time.

"It changes your life," Alison Kaar of LensCrafters says.

LensCrafters chief executive officer Dave Browne, who has challenged his company to help a million needy people by 2003, likes to tell the story of the exceedingly nearsighted schoolteacher in Mexico.

"How did you see your students?" the volunteer asked in wonder.

"I just got to know them by their voices," the man answered.

Charity begins at home, of course. And LensCrafters would like for me to tell you that they provide new eyeglasses to tens of thousands of schoolchildren here in this country, and do free screenings and adjust glasses in senior centers. But if you consider yourself a citizen of the world, if you have connected with any of the photos you've been seeing of Kosovar refugees, think about it.

GOS needs all kinds of glasses, including sunglasses—prescription and just UV-protected. Many mission countries are sunny, and sometimes GOS can't help. They might need surgery or maybe they just don't need corrective lenses. They would be turned away empty-handed. In front of their neighbors.

"We want to keep their dignity," GOS director Susan Knobler says.

Dignity. Sight. Courtesy of you.

If you don't have prescription eyeglasses to donate, give them your old sunglasses. You know, the ones that you thought would make you look just like Tom Cruise in Risky Business. Instead, you looked more like a praying mantis. Take them to any LensCrafters location or give them to a Lions Club member.

Remember how good it feels to find your glasses after you've lost them? Multiply that by about a thousand. That will be how good it feels to somebody who finds your glasses on his nose and is able to see.

For the very first time.

—May 1999

 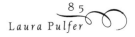

The Real Social Security

JAMES FOX KNEW SOMETHING WAS WRONG as soon as he opened his bank statement. There, as bold as you please, was $44,004 he knew he didn't have. "I thought the bank had made a cruel mistake."

Mr. Fox, 90, thought it was worth the effort to visit the bank in person. "I've been going there for years," he says, "and the teller knows me real well." They shook their heads and agreed. It must be a mistake.

She checked his account and found that the deposit had been made by the U.S. Government, the Social Security Administration to be exact. Besides his monthly check, which is deposited directly by the agency, there was this other one. For $44,004.

"Maybe they've got me mixed up with somebody else," he told the woman at his bank.

He went home and called the Social Security office. He got a "very nice lady." She put him on hold. For a long time. Then she came back, apologized. And put him on hold again. For a longer time.

He waited.

When she came back, she told him that it was a mistake all right. But it had been made in 1974 by some clerk at the Social Security Administration. They had been underpaying him for twenty-four years. The error had been found during a random audit.

"Sir," she said, "it's your money."

It couldn't hurt to double check, he told himself. "I sure didn't want to spend it, then have them say I had to give it back." So, the next day, he called the number again, getting another clerk. She was not, shall we say, as thorough as the first one.

She told him it was most certainly a mistake and that he should immediately write a check for $44,004 to the Social Security Administration.

"Couldn't you just make sure?" Mr. Fox asked politely. He spent a little more time on hold.

Flustered, the clerk got back on the phone and confirmed what he'd been told the day before.

A couple of days later, he got an official letter. The money belonged to him.

He knew exactly what he was going to do with it. He had been hoping to win the lottery—the big one, the Powerball. He even prayed about it, but not for himself.

His 95-year-old cousin could use some help. In his opinion, she shouldn't be living on her own anymore. She needs, he says, to be in a nursing home but can't afford one.

Now she can.

James Fox says he has most everything he needs. He lives in a comfortable retirement village, has seven kids, is surrounded by beautiful watercolors painted by his late wife, Rose Ann. A little stooped by age, he can straighten up after he walks around a bit.

He worked for decades to get what he has. After he lost his job as a lithographer during the Depression, he started selling candy out of his car to mom and pop stores in Corryville, east of Vine. He worked seven days a week. Then he served in the Air Force during World War II and had to start all over again when he got home.

Are you up-to-here with election campaign smears? Have you just about had your fill of sleaze? Would you like some relief from all the bad stuff? Crime, violence, greed? Me too.

I thought you might like to hear some good news, even if it happened to somebody else. James Fox. He got a great big windfall from a most unexpected source.

Then he gave it to somebody else.

—October 1998

J.J.'s Babies An Endless Gift

ONE WOMAN. JUST ONE. She had this idea that she might be able to do something for the kids in her neighborhood. Her neighborhood is Madisonville, and things were not good.

It was right after a shooting, nearly ten years ago. "The neighborhood was polarized," she says. "Black and white." The woman, J.J. Johnson-JioDucci, is a little on the color-blind side herself. OK, very color blind. And very determined.

A bank executive, she takes me into her office to show off pictures of her "babies." Graduations, birthdays, just hanging out. "Nadia, dean's list at OSU. Noran, Mount St. Joseph this fall. Jacob, majoring in zoology," goes her running commentary.

Success stories.

J.J. did not give birth to these children. She has simply claimed the right to care about them. "I grew up in Avondale at a time when everybody took care of everybody," she says.

So it wasn't much of a stretch to fork over $25 to get the same thing going in her new neighborhood. That was the seed money for Students Concerned About Today and Tomorrow (SCATT). The half-dozen charter members met at least once a week, sold candy door-to-door and raised $600 in four months—in time for Christmas of 1991.

They bought a community Christmas tree, toiletries and canned goods for the needy. Since then, new "classes" have adopted a park, made a video, written a book, traveled to Chicago and Washington, attended countless lectures—voluntarily—and just generally made themselves useful.

They are a familiar sight in the neighborhood in their purple and white T-shirts. And a comforting one. One project was taking their elderly neighbors out to dinner. "A lot of the seniors were terrified of young people," J.J. says. SCATT-sters raised the money, picked out a nice restaurant. They dressed up to escort their dates.

"Respect," J.J. says. "They were learning respect." And discipline, I am guessing.

J.J., at age 42, is not their pal. She is a grown-up influence. They call her Ms. J.J. or Ms. JioDucci. They notice that she has a fancy job with a big company. She will be pleased to tell them how that came about.

Hard work. Education.

It doesn't always mean college. J.J., who graduated from Withrow High School and Xavier University, is no academic snob. One of her first "babies," Matthew, still calls her, sometimes on his cell phone, sometimes hanging from a scaffolding. "He always wanted to work with his hands," she says.

"If I ever need to be set straight, I know I can call you," he wrote in a tribute to her, assembled by the kids. She is stepping down from her post as volunteer director of the group. But "they know where to find me."

As these things sometimes happen, if they are ideal, the organization is strong enough to survive without its founder. Maybe even grow. Parents and the kids themselves will take over. College scholarships—two every year—will be wrestled out of candy and garage sales. Some, like Steve, will return to the neighborhood to raise their own babies.

But they will be prepared for that big neighborhood we all belong to, having broken bread with people not their age or their color, having worked to give something to somebody else. They know they can be like Ms. J.J. Successful. A leader. Member of a team. A good neighbor. She is that overworked and generally undeserved term, role model.

If you were standing in the middle of this group of young people—this rainbow of faces—with J.J., you might assume she's a single parent. In a very real way, you would be right. And if you were to ask her which child belongs to her, she would tell you.

All of them.

—May 1999

O l d   C l o t h e s   N e w   L i f e

H<small>AVE YOU STARTED YOUR SPRING CLEANING YET</small>? I haven't, and I say people who already have cleaned their closets and shampooed their rugs are twisted. People who have changed their shelf paper are beyond twisted.

But I'd like to make a deal with everybody who still has work to do, specifically the normal people who haven't yet tackled their closets.

What if your Jones New York jacket—the one that's a little large now that you've been laying off the Graeter's—could help give somebody a new life? It's possible.

It might be somebody who has never in her life needed work clothes because she has never had a job before. But she is ready for one now and your Kasper suit—the one that turned out not to be your color after all—could get her in the door.

Pat Henderson is the manager of a little shop called the Opportunity Closet. Her typical

customer—she calls them "clients"—is a single mother who is right on the edge of going from "welfare to work."

The thing is, this woman has nothing to wear. Really, seriously, nothing to wear. "Some of our clients don't even have bus fare," Pat says. And they sure don't have a good suit for a job interview or anything to wear to work if they get the job.

"They've done the hard part," Pat says. "They're ready to work. But they can't show up in stretch pants and a T-shirt." Besides, when you go out to get a job, you need to feel on top of the world. Valuable.

There are lots of little pieces to welfare reform; this is one of them.

This piece is not costing taxpayers a dime. A bunch of Police Academy recruits came in and painted the walls of what Pat likes to think of as her boutique in the FreeStore/FoodBank center downtown. Some high school boys put up display racks, and three women who have retail experience volunteer as sales consultants.

Except, of course, nothing is for sale. It is free, absolutely free. All a customer has to do is produce a referral from a job training program. They're outfitted for the interview, then they can come back for work clothes if they are hired.

They are treated as though they have a platinum Visa card, with dignity and splendid service. Volunteers pull together entire outfits, including scarves, costume jewelry and new underwear. "They feel great when they see how good they look," says Pat, a pediatric nurse turned volunteer.

Here's the deal. You put the best clothes you have that you can spare in your car and drive down to the FreeStore/FoodBanks collection center at 112 E. Liberty St., downtown. (Don't forget to inventory your shoes, belts and purses.) Pull into the drive-through between 8 a.m. and 5 p.m. Monday through Friday or from 10 a.m. to 2 p.m. on Saturday.

Tell the person on duty that you want your things to go to the Opportunity Closet. Don't forget to ask for a receipt. In addition to more closet space, you can get a tax deduction.

But the real payoff is that this deal includes the certain knowledge that you have sent somebody out into the world dressed to succeed.

—*March 1999*

A Free Store For Teachers

SHOPPERS. CAREFUL SHOPPERS move down the aisles, slowly filling carts. No lookers here, just customers.

The warehouse in Bond Hill is like an office supply store. No, make that a school supply store. It even has the aroma. It smells like crayons. And maybe a whiff of white paste, the kind I used to eat in the first grade when the teacher wasn't looking—until Philip Gerstner told me it was made from the hooves of horses.

Crayons, glue, folders, spiral notebooks, poster board. Then there are the big-ticket items, computers and printers and typewriters. Everything but a cash register.

It's all free.

The shoppers are teachers, bless 'em, on their own time picking up supplies for their classrooms, their kids. They used to pay for stuff like this themselves. Now, all they have to do is make sure the donor gets a thank-you note.

Most come here every week, so they won't miss anything. "We're like Big Lots," says Shannon Carter, president of this place, called Crayons to Computers. "You just never know what will be in the truck."

The trucks arrive filled with computer keyboards, pencils, pens, books, folders, carpet samples, athletic supporters, envelopes—more than a million dollars worth during the first year. Contributors get to take a tax deduction, not to mention the satisfaction of being a good guy.

About a hundred schools meet eligibility requirements, based on the national poverty index. Crayons to Computers serves some of the poorest kids from the neediest schools.

Sister Judy Crooker of Corryville Catholic Elementary School picked up plush bears, slightly irregular, as prizes to reward extra effort, good behavior, attendance.

"These bears were meant for us," a first-grader told her. "They must have known we would love them even if they only have one eye."

Rodney Hughes, a science teacher from Crest Hills Middle School in Roselawn, hit the jackpot. "I found an ionizer," he says, "to put next to one of my kids with allergies."

Science class. Smelly experiments, the aroma of rotten eggs. "That's why I'm always a good customer for their potpourri," Mr. Hughes says.

Geoff Hoebbel, who teaches fifth and sixth graders at Burton Elementary School in Avondale, says he was determined to improve attendance. Calendars, shiny rulers, magnets, stickers. An incentive program. "My attendance went up. Overnight. Drastically. And stayed."

Why, I wondered, haven't we done this before? Everything is right about it. It's the free enterprise system. With an accent on the free and the enterprise. This store interrupts the flow of scrap to the landfill. It gives good teachers the tools they need to do the job, gives kids the basics—and some extras.

The answer may be as simple as the trim woman bustling around the warehouse, straightening piles of notebooks, a smudge of dust on her sleeve. Shannon Carter, who has sold shoes and antiques, who is beautifully dressed, immaculately groomed and impeccably connected, took an idea and made it a cause.

"My kids say I found Jesus in the warehouse," she says, screwing up her face into an unself-conscious grin. She painted walls and scrubbed floors, charmed her friends and squeezed her contacts. She organized and recruited, treating this charity with businesslike respect.

A good idea is never enough. Somebody has to make it happen. That would be Shannon. Somebody has to make it work. That would be Rodney and Geoff and Judy.

And they never forget what this little business really produces: a kid who doesn't have to beg for a pencil and paper.

—*February 1992*

The Paper Monument

THIS IS SOMETHING I'VE BEEN MEANING to do for a long time. I wanted to tell the story of Roy Ketz. It's a good one, even though most of the lawyers and judges in town already know it.

Anybody who has spent time at the Hamilton County Courthouse probably has gotten a greeting card from him, certainly has been asked to sign one. Sometimes you could see lawyers scattering as he approached.

They liked him, but, well, sometimes they had better things to do than sign a greeting card for somebody they barely knew. Plus, who exactly would they bill this time to? Once, Roy said, one of them just came right out and said he was too busy making money.

Roy soldiered on, sending about 130,000 cards over the past forty years. He was a juggernaut of compassion, an antidote to every terrible lawyer joke you've ever heard. Computerized, Hallmark-ized condolences? Ha. He appended personal messages while riding the bus downtown from his home in Bond Hill.

"You a lawyer?" was the way he greeted newcomers. Because, of course, if they were, they qualified to sign one of his cards, which went out to new mothers, new grandparents, the sick, the grieving, the graduates. Roy carried a stack of cards for every occasion.

"He'd catch you everywhere, in the elevator, in the barber chair," Municipal Court Judge Jack Rosen says.

Somebody's kid would break a leg and—bam—a card arrived from Roy. Heart attack? I picture the cardiologist shouting, "Clear. And don't step on the card from Roy Ketz."

How did he know so much so fast? Informants at the hospitals? Spies recruited to his conspiracy of kindness? I am probably making it more complicated than it needs to be. A very nice man, Roy talked to a lot of people.

When Roy Ketz died, people were shocked. "I just saw him." They probably did. He was at work the week before he died, just before he went into the hospital.

A lawyer for more than fifty years, he was probably the guy who stopped to help if you were wandering around trying to find something at the clerk's office. Slightly built, not too tall, he talked fast and had friendly brown eyes.

I always meant to tell Roy's story while he could still read it. And I think of all the people I meant to thank and the birthday cards I meant to send and the notes I meant to write.

That's a problem Roy Ketz never had.

—*March 1998*

 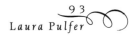

An Overdue Note

A COUPLE OF YEARS AGO, right about now, I received a card from a woman I had never met. She wrote: "Every Thanksgiving, I choose somebody I'm thankful for. This year, It's you."

She said my columns introduced her to a lot of nice people she otherwise wouldn't have met. As is my custom, I shamelessly accepted credit, even though we all know I am merely the typist.

Her note meant so much to me that I decided I would follow her lead, pass that glow on to somebody else the following year. Then I never did it, as is my other custom.

If the road to hell is paved with good intentions, my name surely must appear on most of the bricks.

For instance, I was thinking of sending a note to Joe Hale. President of the Cinergy Foundation, he's a former teacher and now a certifiable Fourth Street suit. I'm not sure exactly what all he does for his company, but I know that it involves giving away millions of dollars after probably zillions of complicated proposals.

Anyway, I told him about a letter from a woman at St. Joseph Children's Treatment Center in Dayton, Ohio, which provides "therapeutic care to the most damaged and violated kids in the community." She said the agency could really use some suitcases for their foster children.

"People may not realize how a simple suitcase could make such a difference for a young person whose life is all about migration," she wrote. "They frequently travel from place to place with their belongings in a garbage bag."

Kids, abused, then shuffled from place to place, probably don't have a lot of stuff. Clothes, maybe some pictures. A book bag. Little kids might have toys. Whatever has survived their various moves must be very dear to them.

Then they have to shove it into a garbage bag. And arrive at the new place, carrying it. How must that feel?

I told myself that I was just chatting with Joe about that letter, thinking aloud about a possible column. It was not what you might call a formal proposal.

That's what I told myself. Even though I knew that two years ago when I wrote about some people who needed a freezer, he fitted them up with a new one. It arrived without a logo on the side, and he didn't send out a news release announcing his good works.

I meant to send him a note.

And didn't.

An hour after I told him about the kids at St. Joseph's, he called to say he had "found" a hundred duffel bags. "Canvas and leather," he said. "They're cool."

Found them, Joe? Along the roadside? In the back seat of your car?

"Hey," he said, "no big deal." He spent an hour or so making calls to see what he could find. And he figured that kids probably would like to arrive at a new destination with a battered suitcase about as much as they'd like arriving with a garbage bag.

Canvas and leather duffel bags. Cool ones.

Hey, Joe, big deal.

Joe Hale is a handsome guy, fit, a runner. He won't mind, I'm sure, if I say that he looks very good in his Fourth Street suit. But I'll bet he never looked better than he did crawling around on his hands and knees with a tape measure, trying to find space for a freezer in the basement of a tenement building. Or fending off a meeting or six while he was shopping for duffel bags.

Dear Joe: Every Thanksgiving, starting now, I choose somebody I'm grateful for. This year it's you.

—*November 1998*

Nine

It Takes A Village To Protect A Nitwit

Neckties And Panty Hose

Don't you wonder what was really behind the revolt in the Netherlands? What could have caused 73-year-old Prince Claus to publicly renounce the innocent necktie in such spectacular fashion?

"A snake around my neck," he snarled, throwing his navy blue necktie at the feet of his wife, Queen Beatrix. And what, I would like to know, was she wearing on the royal feet? This was not reported, although the incident has otherwise been fully explored.

People in Holland are calling it "Claustrophilia."

The *Daily Telegraph* of London reports that it was a "reaction against stuffiness."

Uh-oh. Can Casual Fridays at the Castle be far behind? The king in Dockers and the queen wearing a denim tiara?

Why do men hate ties so fiercely? I thought learning to tie one was a rite of passage, a symbol of guy-ness. A nice tie can disguise the fact that a man is wearing the same suit for two days in a row. Ties are slimming.

"For me, a necktie is like a dog's leash," said a Canadian businessman. "Both symbolize a limit on freedom."

Well, at least it's not a fad. The world's men have had three hundred years to think it over.

Beginning with the cravat, the name given by the French in the reign of Louis XIV to the neck scarf worn by Croatian soldiers, the term came to be applied to a kind of neckerchief worn by a man. When it traveled across the channel to England, of course, it lost all its color.

But it was there that the Windsor knot was invented by the Duke of Windsor after he married Her Skinniness and had no real job to speak of. Historians report that he changed clothes as many as five times a day and had his ties lined for extra plumpness.

He was said to have decreed that "a handsome dimple always distinguishes a properly

tied tie." On the other hand, his countryman, Bond James Bond, said that a Windsor knot was "often the mark of a cad."

A man from Delft said after the public demonstration by Prince Claus that "no piece of clothing combines so little function with so much potential to show bad taste."

"They're a device of torture," a Londoner said.

What a bunch of weenies.

A little rag knotted around your neck is nothing. These men should try to catch a bus wearing three-inch heels. Ask Queen Beatrix how her feet feel after an hour or so in the receiving line.

Women's shoes with high heels or even slightly elevated heels are as obligatory and as stupid and useless as ties. They're not even colorful. And they're expensive. On top of everything else, they're not good for you. Especially if the toes are pointed, which they so often are.

The American Orthopaedic Foot and Ankle Society estimates that up to ninety percent of their patients are women, half of whom have problems caused by their shoes. High heels are also bad for your back, throwing the spine out of whack.

And naturally these shoes cannot be worn without pantyhose, which are the work of the devil. Particularly torturous are those labeled "slightly irregular," which might mean that the feet are pointed in opposite directions. Somewhere on the "slightly irregular" garment is a rogue patch of synthetic thread that will become a tourniquet as soon as you cross your legs.

Pantyhose aren't warm and won't absorb foot odor. They're uncomfortable, costly, fragile, worthless. In short, they are the perfect accomplice for women's shoes.

Thank your lucky stars, Prince Claus. Take another look at that snake lying next to your wife's feet. And be grateful you don't have to walk a mile in her shoes.

—*December 1998*

The Lure Of The Freebie

I DON'T FEEL WELL. IT MIGHT BE INDIGESTION. I think I ate Inspector Gadget's hat. It was dark in the car, and I was desperately hungry.

We were on the way home from a weekend trip with our granddaughter, the Amazing Rosie. When her mother, our daughter, was small, we selected our interstate dining based on the cleanliness of the restrooms. These days, most places have pretty good facilities, most of them with changing tables, some of them with toilet paper.

And I don't care how much fast-food chains spend on their advertising, a burger is a burger. A nugget is a nugget. Grease is grease. The food is pretty much the same. Especially to kids.

So, what separates the drive-through from the drive-by is the quality of their lagniappe. And what, you might reasonably inquire, is an lagniappe? Well, I am pleased that you asked, because I just learned myself and am always eager for the opportunity to show off.

A lagniappe is a fancy foreign-esque word for a freebie. It's pronounced lan-YAP, but you can say it any way you want, because no one will know what you are talking about. For all they know, you are still discussing the restroom using some private family word for something that is too personal to really be discussing with strangers anyway.

Or they might conclude you are merely a pretentious ass.

My well-thumbed copy of Merriam Webster says lagniappe is "a small gift given a customer by a merchant at the time of purchase, something given or obtained gratuitously or by way of good measure."

In the restaurant biz, it used to mean maybe some salsa and corn chips, a stuffed clam "compliments of the chef" or exceptional bread. No big deal and still in the realm of food. Now, you never know what you'll find nestled next to your nuggets. Recently, we patronized Wendy's, where Rosie found a Johnny Bravo bowling game in her bag of food.

I spent the rest of the trip trying to find the little Johnny-shaped bowling pins, which disappeared almost instantly into the crevice of the seat. Or maybe under the floor mat. We know right where the food is. It is still in the bag.

The food is incidental.

The last time McDonald's offered up Teenie Beanies, they didn't even pretend that you came for the food. Many locations had separate tents installed in the parking lots where you could buy the Beanies separately. Adults used cell phones to coordinate purchases with friends.

Now McDonald's is giving away eight toys that form a fifteen-inch Inspector Gadget. I do not have a cell phone, so I was unable to coordinate. We wound up with a torso and a bunch of arms. There was a hat, but as I mentioned, it has come up missing, and I fear for my gastrointestinal tract.

But the thing is, after a while you begin to feel like a patsy if you order food and that's all you get. Everybody else got a nearly naked Tarzan with their fries, and all you got was an extra packet of ketchup.

Just last week, I found myself eating in a little restaurant, even though they did not give me anything except for a really good burger and a couple of napkins.

I asked about their lagniappe, and the kid at the counter said it was down the hall and to the left.

—*July 1999*

Can We Outlaw Stupidity?

CAN WE REALLY PROTECT the world's nitwits? Or, better, protect the world from nitwits? Lord knows we try.

A sign at the gas pump warns us not to breathe the fumes. My laundry detergent instructions tell me not to eat it, and if I'm overcome by a desire for a soap snack, I am told to drink a glass of water or milk.

If I'm not careful with my flea spray, I guess I could end up in prison: "It is a violation of

federal law to use this product in a manner inconsistent with its labeling," warns a can of Vet Kem. I don't even want to know what nitwit is responsible for this label. What do you suppose he did? Spray it on a postal worker? Use it to rob a bank?

We know, of course, why our fast-food coffee cups come labeled with HOT! HOT! HOT! warnings. A LAWSUIT! LAWSUIT! LAWSUIT!

In Beverly Hills, conspicuous consumption capital of the Planet Earth, there is a referendum to require that furs bear a warning label: "This product is made with fur from animals that may have been killed by electrocution, gassing, neck-breaking, poisoning, clubbing, stomping or drowning."

Apparently, some legislator thinks people in ZIP code 90210 would otherwise believe that the pelts come from volunteers. If this passes, I hate to think about what it bodes for the menus at Spago and Morton's. Movie stars might be notified that chickens and cows are not there because they carried donor cards in their wallets.

Up the road in San Francisco, more than thirty self-described "fat rebels" are protesting another kind of label in an ad for a fitness center. The offending billboard pictures a space alien with this caption: "When they come, they will eat the fat ones first."

Both sides of the issue are simply indulging in their constitutional right to express an opinion. We do not discriminate against stupidity. Take, for instance, the things some people believe they need to share with fellow motorists.

Driving in traffic, I came up behind a van with a sign in the window, "Caution, Show Dogs." Maybe otherwise they think we'd say, "Hey, there's no sign on that car. It must just be full of people. Or ordinary dogs. Let's ram 'em."

If drivers would post their cell phone numbers on their bumpers, we could give them a jingle to find out whether they are carrying precious cargo before we sideswipe them. By next year, about eighty million people will be using cell phones in the United States. And eighty-five percent of those who have them now report that they use them while driving.

Some people believe that this poses a greater hazard than show dogs or flea spray. Illinois and Maryland lawmakers are considering restricting the use of car phones. So far, eighteen other states have rejected similar laws. Any sensible person knows phones can be a distraction. So can Rush Limbaugh. So can a toddler demanding to be liberated from her car seat. So can a back-seat driver.

Maybe there's a simple solution. In addition to a vision test when you renew your driver's license, there could be a short Q&A:

"Have you ever applied makeup or shaved while driving?"

"Have you ever read a newspaper while operating a motor vehicle?"

"Have you ever juggled a Big Mac, cola and fries in the speed lane?"

"Have you ever tried to dial your cell phone while changing lanes?"

Those who answer yes would be issued mandatory warning labels: "Caution: Nitwit On Board."

—*February 1999*

Political Dust Buster

AUNT PATTY IS a worrywart.

This is probably not the technical term. I suppose some know-it-all would say she has obsessive-compulsive disorder. As though this is something that needs to be fixed. In fact, it is the Aunt Pattys of the world that keep it turning.

She does not live life on the edge. She simply lives life in advance. Without compromise.

It is not worth mentioning that she already has her Christmas shopping finished. Her table is set and shrink-wrapped. She has already drawn up her gift list for next year and will be hitting the after-Christmas sales hard.

She is careful with a buck. She does not borrow money from friends—or strangers. "If somebody gives you money," she has always warned her children, "they think they can tell you how to spend it." She likes living life on her own terms, which are more exacting than almost anybody else's terms.

An old-fashioned homemaker, she nonetheless is alert to the benefits of modern technology. She microwaves fearlessly and experiments tirelessly with the latest cleaning products.

Living life in advance is not limited to Christmas shopping and cleaning things that are not yet dirty. Her point is that you just can't allow dirt to get the upper hand. It's not good

enough to just clean up afterwards. You have to think ahead. Even if it spoils your fun.

If she'd been anywhere near the White House, she would have been the one to say, "Watch out for that Lewinsky girl. Her skirts are too tight."

She'd have washed James Carville's mouth out with soap and explained to him that he did not elevate his boss or further his cause by calling Paula Jones "trailer trash."

My aunt would have taken Dick Morris' measure in an instant. "He looks shifty and talks out of both sides of his mouth."

She is not one to mince words. Or to twist them.

Hard money? Soft money? "Money is money," she would have told Vice President Gore. Controlling legal authority? "What will the neighbors think?" has been a good enough test for most of life's temptations.

By now, of course, we know what "the neighbors think." At Madame Tussaud's waxworks in Sydney, Australia, they had to sew up the fly of the trousers on the wax figure of the President of the United States.

"People have been taking liberties with his clothing," fumed Vicky Brown, general manager of the exhibition.

Before Ms. Brown ordered the zipper sewn shut, security guards had to check on the state of Mr. Clinton's trousers every couple of hours to "avoid embarrassment."

This, of course, is a case of art imitating life.

Aunt Patty doesn't think this is funny. She still thinks grown-ups ought be behave themselves at the office. She is embarrassed and troubled by every scandal coming out of Washington.

Maybe Aunt Patty could be persuaded to enter public life. Her business card would read: Campaign Finance Chair and Chief Worrywart.

—*December 1998*

Ten

Mending A Broken Heart

Bad News From Good People

MORNINGS ARE NOT MY BEST TIME. I hate to get up. When I smoked, at least I could look forward to that first cigarette. Now, it's just instant coffee.

Oh, and Cammy Dierking.

Alongside the excellent and gentle John Lomax, she anchors WKRC-TV's morning news with acceptable cheer. No giggling. No chirping. I find myself returning her very good smile, even though I'm in my underwear with no cigarette and coffee brewed in the microwave, staring at the screen, listening to the awful things people did to each other during the night.

In 1990, the dependable smile faltered. Her mother, Susan, died just two weeks before Cammy gave birth to her first child.

"My mom went through the whole pregnancy with me." Actually, we all did.

I can remember Cammy, looking a little puffy in the late months, talking about the wait. Then, I think they announced it on the air. Kylee Susan. A beautiful little girl, eight pounds, nine ounces. Perfect.

Three months later, she was dead. SIDS.

It only happens to other people.

"Isn't that silly," Cammy said, "That's what I thought. You never think it's going to happen to you or anybody you know. I just ached for that weight, you know, in the crook of your arm. And her smell. That baby powder smell."

A Sycamore High grad who went just up the road to college at Miami, Cammy could not stand to be here any more, "grieving publicly." She and her husband, John, went to Reno for two years. Their daughter, Whitney, was born there.

"I got my feet back on the ground and was ready to come back." Two more daughters were born here. Cammy does what every mother does, but maybe more often and more fiercely. She goes into her girls' rooms at night and holds her breath to see if she can hear theirs.

She sniffs. I snuffle. We laugh at ourselves and, both without a tissue, dab at our eyes with matching wads of toilet paper. "I thought that I would never be normal again, never be happy. But my kids have given that back to me."

After years of hearing people say they don't want to read bad news, I think I finally understand. You don't want us to stop telling you about fires and plane crashes. You're not suggesting—at least I don't think you are—that we hide things from you. You'd just like to see some light at the end of the tunnel.

You'd probably appreciate it if we looked harder for good news. I'm sorry, but sometimes the news is bleak. Bad. Here is something: If you ever feel so low that you wonder if you'll ever smile again, watch Cammy Dierking.

There's hope.

—March 1996

A P r i c e l e s s L i f e

HELEN MATJE LIVES MODESTLY in a tidy little house in Mount Washington, though she has given away tens of thousands of dollars. Payment from people she holds responsible for her daughter's death, it was not money she wanted to keep.

On Nov. 20, 1981, Kathy Matje committed suicide in jail, hours after she was convicted of drug trafficking. A registered nurse, she said she was set up by an undercover narcotics informant. She told her family and friends she could not bear the thought of being in jail.

Kathy, 32, had no criminal record. She did not hang around with criminals, not counting the Regional Enforcement Narcotics Unit (RENU) informant who testified against her. Louis J. Kahn, according to Kathy's testimony at her trial, asked her to keep a package of Quaaludes for him. She said he had shoved her around and she was scared of him.

Six months after her death, Mr. Kahn was sent to jail for manufacturing drugs, receiving stolen property and intimidation. This was in connection with other cases. Kathy's case was closed.

Except to her mother, of course.

Helen Matje sued.

She went after Hamilton County jail officials, who had been warned that her daughter was suicidal, and RENU, claiming that their negligence led to her daughter's death. She won, sort of.

In 1984, she settled out of court for $130,000 and a list of limits on the way RENU can use informants like Louis Kahn. For instance, informants are prohibited from using force or threat of violence, illegal searches, tapping phones, tampering with the mail.

This was, of course, much too late for Kathy Matje, that "darling girl, so sweet, so much fun to be around." At least this is her mother's description.

But you know how mothers are.

Then she shows me a photo of Kathy in her nurse's uniform. A young woman with pretty features, long shiny hair and an open face smiles out at me from a gold frame. Perhaps I'm seeing too much in a photo because I like her mom and because I think Kathy's death was so tragic and wasteful, but this looks like somebody special.

Somebody irreplaceable. Certainly not replaceable by money.

And isn't that something you'd like to hear these days? Don't you wish, for instance, that Ron Goldman's parents would refuse to touch O.J. Simpsons money?

The family of Lorenzo Collins, the man who was shot and killed after waving a brick at police, is suing the city and the University of Cincinnati for $10 million. Wouldn't it be refreshing to hear that they're doing this to punish and send a message, that when the money rolls in, they're going to use it to help other mental patients?

Helen Matje gave the money she got from the county to the Civil Rights Litigation Fund for victims of things such as employment discrimination and other kinds of civil rights abuses and brutality. She is a retired secretary, widowed a few years before Kathy died, living on a fixed income. She says she never wanted the money from the county, but she wanted to "get back at the idiots who let this happen to Kathy."

Her attorney, Alphonse Gerhardstein, says she could have gotten a bigger settlement if she hadn't insisted on the rules for the drug enforcement agency.

But, of course, Helen Matje meant it when she said that her daughter was precious to her, that no amount of money would ever replace her oldest child.

"That money came from Kathy's death. I wanted to use it to help other people. That's the way she lived her life."

She looks steadily at me, blue eyes magnified just a little by the thick lenses of her glasses. Soft voice. Sad smile. She is taking a chance on this day, dredging up the ugliness again at my request. She still is angry sometimes. And she wants people to know Kathy Matje was a good nurse, a good daughter and a good person.

Priceless.

And she has given us every reason to believe her.

—*May 1997*

Facing A Killer

WHEN THE WOMAN FINALLY LOOKED into the eyes of the man who murdered her only child, tears started rolling down her face. A trickle. Then a flood. She didn't bother to wipe them away, didn't even notice.

She had been waiting for this moment for seven years. Seven years of autopsy reports and police transcripts. Scrambling for information in the middle of a nightmare. A guilty plea, so no trial. And no details.

"I never really knew exactly what happened to my boy. Or why."

They sat—this woman and the prisoner—in a tiny room, on either side of a narrow table. "We could have reached across that table and touched each other," she says. But they didn't.

She pushed a photograph of her son across the table. "I wanted him to know what he took from me."

Everything.

"I'm sorry." The man looked shocked. He hadn't planned to say that. "I think about this every day of my life."

She was not interested in how it made him feel. "You have not told me anything," she insisted. "Tell me what happened that night."

And then he told the woman the details of her son's murder. He was looking for someone who'd stolen money from him, he said. He got the wrong guy. Mistaken identity, he said.

The man yelled at her son, who was sitting in the car she had given to him just a few days before—on his twentieth birthday. When the youth didn't reply, just stared at him blankly, the man shot him. Then he ran away.

She believed every word she was hearing. "I was digging for something in his eyes. I think you can tell when somebody is lying to you when you look at their eyes. Besides," she says, "his story was just so sick it had to be real."

He didn't have to talk to her. Ever. Their conversation, an elaborately choreographed meeting, is part of Ohio's Victim-Offender Dialogue program. And before anybody's conservative knee jerks, it is not for the benefit of the offender.

It is for the victim.

The felon has to agree to participate. No pressure. No incentives.

In eight years, when this man is up for a parole hearing, the meeting with his victim's mother will not be part of the record. He will not be able to point to this moment as proof that he is repentant. Or rehabilitated.

"I will never be a grandmother now," the woman told her son's murderer. "You took that away from me. I go to work. Go to church. I don't have any other life. You took my spirit."

Can I tell your story?

"You can but please don't use my name. I just cannot stand the thought of my name or my son's on another murder story. I don't want to be in the spotlight anymore. I am trying so hard to heal."

She thinks maybe it has started.

—*August 1998*

Eleven

Giving Up Was Never An Option

Laura Pulfer

Looking For Mary Love

THEY ARE LOOKING FOR MARY LOVE, tramping through yet another woods. But the professional searchers have stopped calling the little girl's name. She has been missing more than a week.

Other places have been searched—the woods behind her home, storage areas, a cornfield, back yards. Officials chased a tip to an apartment complex a few miles from where the 6-year-old disappeared.

"Hold on Mary," reads a sign on a neighbor's apartment. "Help is on the way." Pink ribbons. Posters.

You talk about nightmares. This is it. This child didn't come home for dinner, has disappeared. Two days later, members of Hamilton County's new Urban Search and Rescue Task Force were pushing through underbrush and sliding down muddy gullies in Triple Creek Park. Very businesslike. And very quiet.

Steve Ashbrock, leader of the search, says carefully that they are looking for clues in the disappearance of Mary Jennifer Love, three feet tall and weighing forty-eight pounds. "She was wearing a pink bathing suit," the searchers are told before they begin. "We have no reason to believe that has changed."

Such a little person and so much ground, one hundred ten acres this time, including a couple of abandoned houses and maybe an abandoned well. It's rough terrain. The sun is warm but not hot. It's a beautiful day, the sky impossibly blue, clouds white and fluffy. It seems disrespectful. This is a dark time.

The search team works from a grid mapped out minutes before on a laptop computer. They are carrying cell phones and walkie-talkies. Compasses hang from their necks on red cords, and some are wearing bottles of water strapped to their backs. The search plan is on a magnetic board behind the area outlined in yellow crime scene tape.

Command post? This is, I think, just a media-free zone. The waiting is long and the reporters many.

"We've interviewed everybody but the dogs," one said. I am not proud. I look for the dog. But the dog is out in the field with the other searchers, not for the first time.

Mary Love's grandmother, Jeanette Love, arrives at the park. One of the men comes forward to talk to her. He spreads his hands. Nothing.

"They are going to brief me in a few minutes," she says.

"Yes, I am still hopeful." She is not weepy or dramatic. Just tired. She hasn't slept much.

"I think it must have been someone Mary knows," Ms. Love says. "She would not go with a stranger. She knows better."

Present tense.

Jeanette Love is nobody's fool. Her narrow eyes are wise, shaded by a blue ballcap. Retired from T.J. Maxx, where she was a district secretary, she is the organizer of volunteers—uncles, cousins, neighbors and strangers. She has fourteen grandchildren. Fourteen, she says firmly. Counting Mary.

The professionals know what they know. "The sheriff's department is processing a ton of leads," a spokesman says. The grandmother—an amateur—keeps looking, putting more miles on her white Fila sneakers, passing out more posters.

And sometimes she calls Mary's name.

—*July 1998*

Note: A neighbor, one of many who joined in the search, finally led the police to her body. He was tried and convicted of her murder.

The Habitual Hero

IF I'M EVER TRAPPED IN A BURNING BUILDING, I want somebody just like Paula Duncan Anderson to be assigned to rescue me. She wouldn't give up until she carried me out. She'd chop down the door and crawl through the black smoke. She'd beat back the flames and dodge the collapsing walls until she found me.

Or die trying.

At least I think she would. I didn't know her, but I feel like I did. Her smile and baseball cap became as familiar as her name.

For more than a year, people all over town were flipping cheeseburgers, serving up vats of chili, selling cookies and doing just about anything else we could think of to keep this woman alive. Cincinnati City Councilman Charles Winburn donated part of his 1995 salary increase. So did Todd Portune.

Some prisoners at Lebanon Correctional Institution took up a donation to help her battle breast cancer. City workers gave up vacation time. There was even something called a Late-Night Gospel Skate in her honor.

We really wanted her to win this one.

"She was a fighter, and it's good that she's resting now," her husband, Tim, said. Resting was not what she did best. In 1984, Paula and two others were the first women hired by the Cincinnati Fire Division.

"There were sixty-one of us in the class," a male classmate said. "But at the academy, Paula faced real day-to-day challenges unlike the rest of us. You know, can she cut it? Can she carry the dummy? Can she climb the ladder?

"All of this with the media staring down her throat, along with some old-timers in the department who were saying, 'Omigod, a woman.' But the way she handled it, she more than proved herself to everyone there."

Mothers and Other Heroes

Ten years later, another challenge. Breast cancer. Worse, it had spread to her lymph nodes.

She decided, even though the odds were not terrific, to go for broke. After surgery and several rounds of standard chemotherapy, she wanted a bone marrow transplant.

Her doctors told her this was her best chance, and the sooner the better.

The city's insurance company refused to pay for her treatment. She wasn't sick enough yet.

She must have had a good laugh about that. Because there's nothing like a good round of chemotherapy to make you feel as if you're about as sick as you ever want to be. And she was asking for more. The reason she needed the bone marrow transplant was that doctors told her that she should take even more chemotherapy, a dose so lethal that she'd need new bone marrow to survive.

Ever been seasick? Or had food poisoning? Now imagine how much courage it takes to know that you'll feel that bad—and worse—for days, even weeks. That's what Paula Duncan Anderson was agreeing to do.

I remember thinking that I might be tempted to just pack it in. Quit. Then I saw pictures of her with her daughter, Jasmine, 4. And I understood. She also has older children, a son, Darrell, and another daughter, Danielle. She wasn't just fighting for her own life.

I also understood why, after the cancer came back, invading her spine and lungs, she fended off morphine.

"My goal is to spend as much time with my kids as possible," she told a reporter. Time unclouded by drugs, if she could help it.

Paula Duncan Anderson, just 34 years old, died last week. I think we can assume that she never really gave up. And the reason seems clear. Her last assignment, one she accepted with heroic grit, was to mother her kids.

And she died trying.

—April 1996

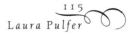

Waiting For A Miracle

REALLY, I DON'T THINK THE STORY COULD have been more dramatic. A little boy snatched from the home of his prominent parents. FBI. Series of ransom calls. A daring, and I mean daring, rescue. Don't you love a happy ending? Boy, I do.

Jason Comisar, kidnapped eighteen years ago, now is a senior at Miami University, a good-looking kid, an inch or three under six feet. "No ill effects," reports his father, Michael E. Comisar, over coffee at the family's Maisonette restaurant.

Now president of the Maisonette Group, Michael was only 27 years old in 1978 when a man broke into the Comisars' North Avondale home, pointed a pistol at Kathy Comisar and demanded money. Just then, their 3-year-old son awakened from his afternoon nap and toddled into the room.

Bruce Nelson Baltzer, son of an affluent businessman, grabbed the naked little boy by the hand and ran out of the house.

Michael "drove home at about a hundred miles an hour, then there was nothing for me to do." Except wait.

The hours passed in "sort of a shock state," but Michael Comisar can remember when he first met FBI agent Jim Ader. "He was very reassuring. Ader was the lead guy—the get-the-kid-back guy." Middle-of-the-night phone calls from the kidnapper, who faked a heavy French accent, demanded that $100,000 be left in a briefcase at the airport.

Mr. Comisar made the drop the morning after his son's abduction. Bruce Baltzer retrieved the money, then shoved the boy, still naked, out of his car. When the kidnapper spotted Jim Ader running toward him, he gunned the car straight toward the agent.

Mr. Comisar says, "Jim stood right there." He mimes a two-handed crouch stance. "He shot. He spun out of the way and shot again."

Then this tough guy, this authentic tough guy, found a white blanket and wrapped the

child in it. He buried his face briefly in the little boy's mop of hair, I am told, before he picked Jason up and carried the child home to his mother.

A year or so later, Jim Ader was transferred to another FBI office. Bruce Baltzer was convicted and sent to jail. He was paroled, tried to rob a Kroger store and died in prison. Meanwhile, the FBI agent captured more than three hundred fugitives and rescued five more kidnapped children before his retirement in January 1994.

A friend here in Cincinnati remembers him as "a health nut, always keeping in shape and eating right. So it seems doubly unfair that this should happen to him."

"This" is a congenital liver disease, primary sclerosing cholangitis. His only chance is a liver transplant. Jim's wife, Sheila, talking to me from Tucson, said, "Please don't make this a sob story, something pitiful. Jim would hate that."

Well, of course, I have absolutely no control over anybody else's tear ducts. But, myself, I think the whole thing is rather touching.

"He doesn't want any special favors or anything," his wife says. I sort of knew that, because Michael Comisar says Jim Ader won't even let him pick up the tab at LaNormandie when he's back in town.

"After the testing and confirmation that we have financing, Jim's records will go before a committee," Sheila says. "The transplant committee does not just review medical information, but tries to learn what the candidate was in life."

So, anyway, Jim Ader, this good and brave man, is in Tucson. Waiting for a happy ending.

—*April 1996*

Note: Shortly after this was written, Jim Ader received a successful liver transplant. He is healthy and works tirelessly as a volunteer for various national transplant programs. He has personally counseled dozens of transplant patients. Still, an authentic hero.

Lunch With Ernie

MY FRIEND ERNIE WAITS and I have lunch together every once in a while. We spend a little bit of time figuring out which restaurant we'll choose. I'm usually negotiating to keep my feet dry, and he's trying to decide where he'll be able to find a parking space.

We do not have to wonder if we will be permitted to eat there. It would not occur to us that we wouldn't be seated. Or served. At least, it wouldn't occur to me. People in my generation have short memories. Sometimes we are ungrateful to boot. We are, finally, getting around to noticing the gallantry of the generation before us.

"Suddenly, baby boomers realize that despite a buzzing economy, we are going to die without experiencing the nobility that illuminated the lives of our parents and grandparents," writes columnist Maureen Dowd.

Well, that sounds very fancy.

And probably nothing like the inside of, say, the old jail at Ninth and Central. Or being told your kids couldn't go to Coney Island. Or being turned away from the Albee or the Shubert theaters.

Ernie tells me about the time in 1939 when Eddie "Rochester" Anderson from the Jack Benny show was coming to the Shubert. "I thought they couldn't—wouldn't—keep me out when there was a black artist on stage," he says. "So I show up, dressed to the nines, first at the window."

The man selling tickets refused to sell one to Ernie. The police were called. Mike Bizzari, who was a classmate of Ernie's at Woodward High School, was in line with his wife, Jane.

"I saw the police grappling with Ernie," Mike says. "I told 'em that the guy was a friend of mine. So they said I should come down to the police station the next day and vouch for him."

Which he did.

"It was an awful thing to see," says Mike, who lives now in Mason. "And I never forgot it."

Ernie, who had been charged with resisting arrest and disorderly conduct, got out of jail and a week later was at the door of the Albee Theater. Several years later Nat King Cole played there to a big crowd, black and white.

Progress.

Still, Mr. Cole was taken afterward to the Manse Hotel, owned by a black man. The Gibson was off-limits.

"It was a fight," Ernie says. "It was a struggle. It was constant."

Looking at Ernie, with his enormously kind face and gentle manner, it's hard for me to imagine him butting heads, sometimes literally, with anybody. But then it was always hard for me to imagine my dad as a soldier.

Besides being a troublemaker, Ernie was the first black investment counselor here and the first disc jockey to put music by black artists on mainstream radio. Now he says he is a "retired contract compliance specialist and employment consultant."

I tell him that is gobbledygook for "holding people's feet to the fire until they obey the law." And that I do not believe he has retired.

My generation is in a frenzy of admiration just now, for our parents. We love Tom Brokaw's book "The Greatest Generation" and Steven Spielberg's movie *Saving Private Ryan*. The Great Depression. The Battle of the Bulge. Veterans Day. Selma, Ala. Martin Luther King Day. We're in the mood for heroes and, of course, nobility of all kinds.

Nobility? I am going to ask Ernie to have lunch. That way, I can look right across the table and see it.

—*January 1999*

Winning The Human Race

FOR YEARS, I HAVE SCOFFED AT WOMEN who run. They pound along the pavement, rain or shine, hauling in great lungs full of bad air, dodging traffic and dog poop. What can they be thinking? I suspect they run so they can eat chocolate and cheesecake without becoming

dirigibles. I assume their doctor—or their movie of the week—has thrown some kind of cardiovascular scare into them.

You are going to jar your innards loose, I would tell my friends. Your uterus is going to fall out, and you will trip over it and break your neck. How can this be good for you? And what about your knees?

"Well, what about your own knees?" someone might have replied. "they are getting to be the size of hubcaps. Maybe you should use them for something besides propelling you to the head of the buffet line."

Of course, nobody actually said that to me. But they could have. Then I would have said that in the unlikely event that I did decide to try to get in shape, I certainly would choose something that was more fun. Tennis. Golf. Alligator wrestling.

You rarely see anybody running who looks as if they're having a good time. Scowling and bobbing at traffic lights, they mostly look as if they are on their way to have a boil lanced. I have asked Julie Isphording about this more than once. This is probably not fair because she is hardly the average runner. A member of the 1984 U.S. Olympic team, Julie has always run with visible joy, a picket-fence smile.

She has continued to spring along the sidewalks of Cincinnati after being bitten by dogs, flashed by a pervert and hit by a bus. She has suffered countless injuries and back surgery three times. Still she runs.

She says it feels like flying. I can only imagine her anguish when she thought it was lost to her. Without warning, one of her legs would buckle. Multiple sclerosis was a possibility. Still, she ran, falling, "bandages on my knees." Every day is better. "I have run now for 110 days, and every one is a gift." She does not have multiple sclerosis, thinks the problem is related to back injuries. Whatever it is, she is nearly giddy with what she calls "the joy of movement."

I still don't get it, I tell her. Running feels to me as though I am jarring my back teeth loose.

Julie looks around for moral support. On cue, Kathrine Switzer appears. Winner of the 1974 New York Marathon, she looks the way most women I know would like to look. Trim. Glossy dark hair. Luminous skin. And something more. She looks as if she knows where she is going.

In 1967, Kathrine broke the gender barrier in the Boston Marathon. One race official

literally tried to throw her out of running. "He actually grabbed me, ripped my number off," she says. "Male runners have always been very supportive. They are not threatened by women. The officials have been a different ballgame."

So now, she is an official herself. Program director for Avon's Global Women's Circuit. Which is for women only. After breaking one gender barrier, why is she setting up another one?

"The fastest woman will never beat the fastest man. We can run longer, endure cold better. But men have more lean muscle and bigger lungs. This race is a chance for women to cross the line first, break the tape."

Breaking the tape. Getting there first. Winning. Everybody should have that feeling at least once. Somehow.

I am watching two women who know the feeling—Julie Isphording, who slipped out in the dark trying to run again without falling, and Kathrine Switzer, who says her mission is to give every woman a nudge to be healthy and fit—stride through the lobby of an elegant hotel.

They walk with a certain bounce, even on a marble floor. This surely has something to do with genetics, something to do with running. And something to do with breaking the tape.

—August 1999

Twelve

The Opposite Of Mom Is Dad

Laura Pulfer

Coming A Short Way, Baby

SOME WOMEN—AND I'M EMBARRASSED to point this out—are still saying, "You've come a long way, Baby." Aloud. In public. They must have forgotten that this slogan came from a cigarette manufacturer, basically urging women to challenge male domination in the area of lung cancer and heart disease.

Another more recent television commercial, shot in bleak black and white documentary style, shows men in a bar discussing their bodies. "Do these pants make my butt look big? I hope not," one says mournfully, his moon eyes looking directly into the camera.

"I have my mother's thighs. I'll have to accept that," another declares manfully.

It's very funny, but I can't remember what they are trying to sell. I asked some of my friends. One thought it was breakfast cereal. One was sure it was an ad for hair dye. Somebody else thought it might be a come-on for a diet plan or health club. I myself seemed to remember a pitch for orthopedic shoes.

(Note to advertising client: Ask for your money back.)

In any case, my friends and I all remembered the message, aimed at women: "Men don't obsess about these things. Why do we?"

Well, there is compelling evidence that men do worry about these things. Otherwise why are they drinking lite beer and working out on the Nautilus ab machines? I do not think this is because they are concerned about cardiovascular health. If fat didn't show, they wouldn't care if they had it.

According to the American Society of Plastic and Reconstructive Surgeons and the American Society for Aesthetic Plastic Surgery, the number of men having cosmetic surgery has increased sixty-four percent since 1994. About ninety-nine thousand men underwent cosmetic surgical procedures in 1998. And it's not just hair plugs. Men are having love handles liposuctioned, noses bobbed and eyelids nipped. They're going under the knife to have male breast-reduction surgery, known as gynecomastia, and the new shorter hairstyles have increased the number of men seeking otoplasty, which is medical-ese for having their ears pinned closer to their heads.

Some of them are having pec implants. A Harvard psychiatrist thinks action dolls are to blame, much in the same way that Barbie has been accused of encouraging girls to believe they should have tiny waists, enormous breasts and pathologically high arches.

Dr. Harrison Pope said the beefy GI Joe Extreme doll, if he were calibrated to human dimensions, would have twenty-six-inch biceps. That is eight inches bigger than Barbie's waist if she were similarly scaled. The doctor suggests this could encourage boys to devote themselves to a dangerous quest for ever more bulging lats and delts and pecs.

"Before the 1960s, people weren't using anabolic steroids, so men would lift weights and stay within their natural body size," said Dr. Pope, "but now the unnatural is possible."

Speaking of which, a British fertility expert said male pregnancy is less than ten years away. The next thing you know, men will be forming support groups to be allowed to nurse their babies in public. They will be on the Mommy track and bumping their heads on a glass ceiling.

Women, I suppose, will be viewing these antics from the corner office. They'll be knotting useless scraps of fabric around their necks and refusing to ask for directions. They will be workaholics who never see their children.

And men will be buff, barefoot and pregnant.

We can look at each other and say, "You've come a long way, Baby."

—*May 1999*

Monuments To A Good Scout

THIRTY-FOUR MEN WITH MOSTLY white hair, or not much hair at all, face the camera squarely. Light bounces off their spectacles. In the front row, a man leans on a walker. The rest stand carefully, an occasional arm thrown over a shoulder. All wear coats and ties and white or pale blue shirts.

 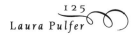

Not to read too much into a photograph, but they look like men who face life squarely as well. And they look like what they are—a bunch of old Boy Scouts. This is their annual meeting.

Scattered all over the country now, they grew up in Clifton, meeting in the Methodist church at Senator Place and Clifton Avenue. After they were mustered out of their Troop 161 at age 18, their Scoutmaster said they would be "assistant Scoutmasters" and could still get together when they wanted.

Which they have been doing for forty-nine years.

"We didn't want to give up Scouting," says D.A. Brown, "or each other." And that is probably about as sentimental as any of them is likely to get. I can't imagine them sitting around inside a sweat lodge or in an encounter group where they would explore their feminine side. Their conversation runs more toward remembering campouts and marching in the Armistice Day parade.

"We are like a bunch of kids in old bodies," one of the men says.

Oh, and they do get a little misty when they talk about their Scoutmaster, Nux, pronounced "Nooks."

"I came from a kind of a broken home," says Dustin Schermbeck. "And Nux kept me going." Alvin S. Boesche was called "Nux" by the women who shopped at his little grocery store on the corner of Woolper and Vine. This was one familiarity he also allowed his Scouts. The rest of it was by the book. Disciplined. A little formal sometimes.

"He didn't have to tell us to get quiet when it was time for the meeting to start," Mr. Brown says. "All he had to do was go to the front of the room."

The "assistant Scoutmasters" remember Nux, dead now for nearly ten years, as a "massive person." Tall with thinning dark hair, he was always impeccably dressed. "He made us work, gave us goals," Mr. Schermbeck says.

Nux taught them how to cook and make campfires. Mr. Schermbeck can "still do the flint and steel in three seconds." That means he can ignite a fire without matches.

Not much call for that these days.

One of the men shakes his head and tells about visiting a Scout camp recently where "one of the kids called his mother on a cell phone."

Eyes roll.

This year, as usual, Troop 161 will gather. They will remember pranks and a time when

they turned their neckerchiefs over so that the BSA for Boy Scouts of America was backwards, ASB for Alvin S. Boesche, a man who was a role model before we knew that's what they were called, somebody who stuck up for kids who came from "sort of a broken home" and who made them shut up and listen when it was time.

There are monuments all over the city to important men. Brass plaques. Buildings. Streets. The monuments to Nux are scattered all over the country. A fireman, construction workers, a couple of doctors, a dentist, accountants, lawyers, all facing life squarely, just as he taught them.

—December 1998

The Legacy Of A Good Life

HE WAS LISTED ON THE VARIOUS letterheads of the institutions he served as Edgar J. Mack Jr. But if you were invited to do so, you could call him Buddy. Otherwise, it was Mr. Mack. There was no in between.

When I first met him, he was only 75, still clobbering much younger men on the tennis court, still riding his horse, still mowing his own lawn. About five years later, we met for lunch. After a few minutes, he asked me if I noticed anything different about him.

This was a hard question, because he was dependably, almost fanatically the same. Iron gray hair swept back from his face, he never looked like he had just gotten a haircut—or that he needed one. His dark suits had never hung on a rack but were tailored for him, as were his crisp cotton shirts. Silk ties, and you could be assured that they would not have hand-painted palm trees on them.

"I give up, Buddy."

He said he had quit smoking after more than six decades. And of course I should have noticed. Until that moment, I don't think I had ever seen him without a cigarette. No longer. He would not have the occasional cigarette after dinner. He would not be chewing Nicorette gum. No tobacco. No in between.

He said his doctor had insisted.

Ha.

His doctor might have convinced him of the wisdom of such a step, suggesting he might live longer or more comfortably. But I cannot imagine that his doctor "insisted." Buddy ran his own life and, occasionally, the lives of others as well.

After the riots of the late 1960s, he headed a city task force charged with rebuilding the West End. He was buttonholed by a woman from that neighborhood. "We need a stop sign," she told him. "It's a dangerous intersection, children coming home from school, somebody is going to get hit. The city won't listen."

Buddy told me he didn't know if the stop sign was important, but he knew it was important to show this woman respect and that he could get things done. "She had a lot of power in that neighborhood," he said.

He "made a few calls." The stop sign went up the next day.

When the Cincinnati Symphony Orchestra was trying—unsuccessfully—to hire the brilliant and charismatic Thomas Schippers as music director, Buddy flew to Milan and brought back a contract. He saw what was needed and went after it. Simple. And complicated. A man of the world whose interests were centered in Cincinnati and its environs.

He grew up in Avondale, the privileged son of the German Jewish founder of Red Top Brewery. Cotillions. Private clubs. Then he went away to school, to Princeton. "Jews were very restricted there," his eldest son, Ted, says. "And my father hated it."

Maybe that's why he opened so many doors to African-Americans and women, "making a few calls," twisting a few arms.

Buddy helped write his own obituary, which appeared in *The Cincinnati Enquirer* reporting his Thanksgiving Day death at the age of 89. Besides his family—the exquisite Elaine, his wife of 68 years, and their children, grandchildren and great-grandchildren—he was proud of the doors opened, the legacies to strangers. He rolled up the sleeves of his handsome shirts, pushing for education and the arts and housing and, well, sometimes simple dignity.

"Buddy didn't measure the odds," says an African-American man Buddy hired when nobody else would. "He just did what he thought was right."

There was no in between.

—December 1998

The Case For Speaking Up

SUCH A CLICHÉ. A tie for Father's Day. My father's closet contained dozens of them I bought over the years.

Well, what would I get him? An electric guitar? Silk jockey shorts? He was a dad, for pete's sake. A good one. And once a year, I would let Hallmark tell him so.

I usually handed him the gift and pre-printed sentiment in person. If I did have to mail it, I always knew the address. The term Deadbeat Dad was not coined for my father's generation. These guys took care of their own, without encouragement from a domestic court referee.

Not all of them. But enough that we didn't have to assemble whole bureaucracies to chase men who owed money to their kids. No government agency has so far been able to figure out how to supply what these children are owed in delinquent personal support.

The real dad stuff.

When we were preparing the death notice for the newspaper three years ago, we were asked a lot of questions about my father. Education. Job. But they didn't ask us enough questions. Or maybe just not the right ones.

They didn't ask: Was your father ever a Little League coach? And did he make sure every kid got to play? Even the ones who dropped the ball every time? Yes, yes and yes.

By the way, did he teach his girl-child to throw a spiral pass? Did he get her a first-baseman's mitt for Christmas? Because that's what he had? Did he work a second job so that she could go to college, even though high school had been plenty good enough for women in his generation?

Of course he did.

Was he a Boy Scout leader? Yes, indeed. Even after his own boys were through being scouts. Even though he'd really had more than enough of sleeping in tents when he was in the Army.

There are lots of pictures of him in his uniform in our photograph albums. But not so many of our nearly fifty years together. Birthdays, weddings, graduations, anniversaries. Photos of me and Mom. Pictures of Mom and my brothers, our spouses and kids. But not many of Dad.

He was the one holding the camera.

Pictures of me on my new Christmas bicycle. But no pictures of him taking off the training wheels, then running behind, holding onto the seat until I could keep my balance by myself. "Don't let go until I'm ready, OK, Dad?"

Did he ever build a treehouse? He did. And all the corners were square and the roof did not leak. Did he let you have a dog? Yep. Was he ever the guy at the party with the lampshade on his head? Not a chance.

I was not Daddy's Little Girl. We fought a lot, especially when I was a teen-ager and knew everything. He was so strict. No alcohol in the house. He never smoked. Naturally, I couldn't wait to do both.

Later, I was smart enough to seek his advice. We had started to talk more. We even had a beer or two together. I admire the way he lived his life, and I wish I'd said so to him—aloud—a cappella. With no musical phrases from Hallmark. I didn't know I was running out of chances.

This one time, Dad, you let go before I was ready.

—May 1999

Thirteen

Hitting The High Spots

Laura Pulfer

Perfect Sight

JUDY SCHLETKER is still running.

A dabbler in the early 1980s when she hooked up with Greg Thiel, Judy began running harder and longer. "He got me my first race," she says, "and gave me lots of advice."

Such as?

She laughs. "Run faster."

Greg can still make people laugh. Even now.

"Hey," he used to tease his friends, "gain another pound and even I will be able to see you."

If only.

Greg Thiel was a runner, a biker, a swimmer and a golfer. He did these without being able to see. Blind. He never saw his wife, Joyce, in her wedding gown or the faces of his two children.

Just 18 years old, working at a job after school, he lost his sight in an industrial accident. A few years later, surgery on one eye allowed him to see long enough to become a massage therapist and meet Joyce. Then he lost it again.

"Scar tissue," Joyce says. They met in 1976 and by the time they married two years later, he was sightless.

"He knew this might happen," she said. "He just looked at it as something that changed his plans a little."

Joyce and Judy met at St. Luke Hospital West in Florence, Ky., where both still are nurses. Ostensibly Judy was Greg's guide. And, indeed, he did hold on to her elbow and keep the rhythm of the run with her braided hair batting his arm.

"I could see," Judy says. "But he knew all the routes." Imagine how brave you must be to run when you cannot see the bumps in the road or the stones or the mailboxes. Imagine how fine a man must be to attract hundreds of people to his side.

Mothers and Other Heroes

Then Greg had a pain in his side that turned out to be cancer. "He had no other symptoms," Joyce says. "He was tanned from vacation. He looked great. And the doctor was saying 'we'll try to make you comfortable.'" He was dead six months later.

During Greg's last weeks, Joyce put out the word, "The door to our house will be open from 8 a.m. to 8:30 p.m." A steady stream of visitors came to their home. They came to comfort him, and "had them all laughing before they left."

When he died in January, he was hugely mourned. There were, of course, clients. People from his church. Runners. Neighbors. Young and old. All colors. Both sides of river. Lines around the block at the memorial service.

This was not a crowd you could assemble in a hurry. It took a lot of being a good guy, years of corny jokes and a stunning example of bravery from this man who lost his sight not once, but twice.

"He'd pull you up," says Geof Scanlon, his friend of twenty-two years. A tribute by Geof in a newsletter for runners reads: "To all friends of Greg who are moving slowly, with sore knees over shorter distances, remember Greg can see you. Just for him, dig little deeper, reach a little higher, run a little harder. The wind at your back is probably he."

Three or four mornings a week, you can see Judy pounding the pavement. She appears to be running by herself. But she is not alone.

—June 2000

Higher Education

THE MOST NEWSWORTHY PORTION of Elizabeth Eichelbaum's story, I suppose, is that at age 90 she earned her doctorate. The title of her dissertation is "The Use of Art Therapy to Deal with Low Self Esteem Among the Aged."

Mrs. Eichelbaum's son, Stan, who runs a consulting firm in Cincinnati, drove to his mother's house just before her graduation from the University of Tennessee in Knoxville. His plan was a succession of wonderful restaurants for out-of-town family meeting him there. Ha.

Elizabeth Eichelbaum cooked. Chicken. Sweet and sour meatballs. Pancakes. "People say I set a nice table. It was only forty or so. I like to do things for myself."

Nearly blind from macular degeneration, she hired students to help during the last two years of her doctoral preparation. She can't drive anymore, so she walks to work at a nursing home. A small journey, she says.

The big journey was from Russia to find her mother, who had come to this country when Elizabeth was 18 months old. "It took a couple of years to save enough money to send for us, and when she did, it was too late. The war had started." Her grandmother, who had been caring for the child, died in a basement where they were hiding from soldiers.

After the war, some American reporters came to Kiev. A little girl in an orphanage told them she had a mother in America. Connection was made. "We started our journey in a covered wagon." A year later, she boarded a ship from France to New York and a tenement in Harlem. She arrived in October of 1921. Her first American shoes were high-top Buster Browns. She cooked. She cleaned. She went to school. She finished the eighth grade, then went to work in a clothing store.

And always she drew pictures.

She married a baker and moved to Detroit, where they owned a Kosher restaurant just a block from the headquarters of Motown Records. Marvin Gaye, Milton Berle, Lenny Bruce were among the regulars.

After her husband died, she went back to school. "When I was young, all a girl had to do was read and write and get married." She passed the GED test with flying—extremely flying—colors and enrolled in college, receiving her bachelor's degree at age 69 and her master's at 81. By now, her drawings have become paintings. "Since I'll have a little more time now, I will be painting more."

And working, of course. Cleaning her house, cooking and bringing her favorite message to the people at the nursing home. "Try it," she tells them. "You might amaze yourself."

Her family has started a scholarship in her name to support other students, a little financial nudge, a reminder that it's never too late. "Don't tell me you can't do something," she would say to her sons, this woman who begged for food as a child and walked on feet scarred by frostbite, who worked twelve- and fourteen- and sixteen-hour days.

Stan thinks his mother's life should be a book called *Growing Young.* And the best lesson is that Dr. Elizabeth Eichelbaum has not yet written the final chapter.

—*May 2000*

N e w   R a c e   F o r   P e t e

PETE STRAUSS, FORMER CINCINNATI vice mayor, interrupts himself three or four times to wave at people, as he tucks into an English muffin and bacon at the Echo in Hyde Park. He is having no trouble with his hands just now. He buttoned the cuffs of his own crisp white and blue pin-striped shirt and tied the tight Windsor knot in his silk necktie. It has been a good morning.

Right around the time of his fiftieth birthday, eight years ago, he tried to make some hand-written notes. And couldn't. Then he started limping. "I'm a little hard pressed to remember the symptoms" he says. "This disease is so unpredictable, things kept changing."

Unpredictable. Parkinson's is also progressive and incurable. Billy Graham suffers from it. So do Muhammad Ali and Pope John Paul II and Janet Reno. And, lately, of course, Michael J. Fox.

"Everybody is different," Pete says. "I never had the tremors. I just—I just would freeze up. My body wouldn't go where my mind told it to. Nothing hurts. My hands just don't work sometimes." He has difficulty walking. He takes eighteen pills a day. Those pills allow him to work, which he is proud to do. He left his law firm two years ago, practices on his own and serves "on a ton of boards." Oh, and he says he's a consultant. By that, I think he means he guides others through the perilous waters of Cincinnati politics, where he swam most of his adult life.

In his twelve years on Cincinnati's city council, he got some things done and tilted at a few windmills. My personal favorite in the latter category was a proposal that any new lease with the Bengals should include a performance clause.

Pete left office in 1993, the victim of term limits. He toiled on the Year 2000 Report and its 1990 revision. He worked on housing, downtown development, campaign reform and zoning. He trolled for votes at bowling alleys and bingo parlors and waved from the back of convertibles during parades. He ate rubber chicken and knocked on doors. "I thought it was fun. I got to know a lot of people. I hope they believed I was always straight up with them."

As we are leaving the restaurant, he automatically moves to put himself between me and the curb—an old-fashioned gesture, much like struggling to his feet when a woman stopped by our table. "Don't get up," she says.

She is wasting her breath.

"A gentleman," says Pete's first political opponent former Hamilton County commissioner Bob Wood. "A hard fighter but a class candidate."

Fellow attorney Kent Wellington says, "He fights for the underdog, isn't afraid to take a stand." And this gallant man—this thoroughly decent public servant—is still fighting, but his race now is against time. He's grateful, he says, that Michael J. Fox has captured the public's attention. "I'm a lot more confident that this disease will be dealt with. It used to be way down on the list."

We parted at the corner, and I watched him make his way down the street. Not looking back. Listing slightly. But very straight up.

—*May 2000*

Going For The Gold

NO WAY WOULD LAURIE PHENIX miss seeing her daughter, Erin, swim in Sydney. The single mom has been there for teething and runny noses and soccer games and scraped knees and, you know, all the basic I-love-my-kid stuff. There for Erin's first swimming lessons at age 8, her mother would hardly miss a chance to see her compete at the Olympics.

It will be a stretch financially. Even with the special parents' package—$3,500 for airfare and hotel during the week's activities—it wasn't exactly the kind of money Laurie had tucked in the cookie jar at her Greenhills home. A lot of things are a la carte. Food is extra. Plus it costs $350 to see an event.

Laurie was proud to send Erin to Ursuline Academy, for a "really good" education. Good but not cheap. Now a sophomore at the University of Texas in Austin, Erin is on scholarship. But it doesn't pay for everything. Phone calls home, for instance.

Essential.

Friends are determined to help. In a material way. They're taking a collection. It's not that Laurie is destitute. She has a good job. Two of them, in fact.

"I figured I can just max out my credit card, then pay it off. For the rest of my life," she says, laughing.

But not kidding. A speech and language pathologist for Cincinnati Public Schools, Laurie also works part-time at a hospital birthing center. Erin's father "disappeared during the pregnancy," she says.

"Her friends watched her raise that baby by herself," says long-time friend Tess Neggerman. "What a wonderful job she has done. Helping her go to Sydney is a way for us to gather around and say 'atta girl.'"

The tough thing about raising children on your own, Tess says, is having somebody else around for the big and small moments, somebody to turn to and say "isn't she smart, isn't she great? Raising this money is a way for all of us to be with Laurie and Erin in Sydney," Tess says. "Send along our good thoughts and prayers."

More prayers. Well, that seems to work so far. Erin says she closed her eyes and asked her late grandmother for one of her famous novenas before plunging into the water at the Olympic trials. Tim Beerman, Erin's coach, was on a religious retreat. "I had all the monks praying for her," he told Diane Redmond, Ursuline's athletic director.

Diane is in charge of the purse, and she reports contributions of $400 so far. "We're going to do this for Laurie. For both of them, really. Laurie has always been there," Diane Redmond says. "Not just for Erin. She helped organize things for the team, dinners when we went to state. An outstanding person. It would be so much fun to be able to take some of the pressure off her."

But whether she gets outside help or she doesn't, Laurie will be there to cheer for her daughter. Just as she always has.

Atta girl.

—*August 2000*

Note: Erin helped her relay team win a gold medal, and Laurie was there, thanks to her friends and neighbors.

Shocking Service From Mystery Clerk

THIS MIGHT NOT BE the biggest economic news of the decade, but I'm hoping it's a trend. I went to a shopping mall to find an electric hand mixer. It doesn't matter where. A mall is a mall. Free parking. Baby strollers in the aisles. Many, many stores. Many, many shoppers. Very little service.

First, I tried the department store at one end—an anchor store I think they call it, perhaps because it appears to be taking on water and going down for the third time. I couldn't find a hand mixer, and I couldn't find a clerk.

The trick is to look for women who are not carrying purses. If you get close enough—and I admit they can run like deer—try to spot a nametag. I cornered one hiding behind a register. She did not know if they stocked any hand mixers, and she was not interested in finding out. "We used to have them," she said.

Another store carried hand mixers you could order from their bridal book. Do brides still know how to fix anything that requires a mixer? There really is no reason to stick a beater into a Wendy's bag and turn it on. Anyway, this was a gift for somebody who had been a bride twenty years ago, so she often serves her family food that originated in her kitchen. And I needed the gift that day.

I ducked into yet another store where a clerk was right out in plain sight, looking as if she'd like to make a sale. I asked about their hand mixer situation, and she led me to the shelf. Then—and I swear to you it happened exactly this way—she took the mixer out of the box to make sure all the pieces were there. Without any encouragement from me. I am not even sure this was technically her area. But she seemed to think that customers were her area.

I followed her up to the register. "Do you gift wrap?" I was making a little joke. If a store offers wrapping, it is done nowhere near the point of purchase. You need a field atlas to find the gift wrap department. Which is where they usually ransom the boxes as well.

She said she had some "kind of awful" paper. I think she meant say to it was "butt ugly," but possibly in deference to my age, or in keeping with the kitchen motif, she called it "bunt ugly."

Other customers were milling around by then, so "this might take little while." It's quicker, I am thinking, than finding the tape at home. "Take your time," I said generously. Time is something she doesn't appear to waste. Doing three things at once. Shutting a drawer with a hip, phone clamped to her ear. Ringing up a sale. A smile that went all the way to her eyes.

Hasn't missed a day in two years, she says. Juggling a couple of kids and day care. From welfare to work.

Did I mention that I spent another $50 while she was using up that bundt ugly paper? I promised not to tell her name because wrapping is not part of the service and she's afraid she might get in trouble. So, if you think you might be her boss, my advice is to give her a big raise.

Because you are lucky to have somebody like her, somebody grateful for a job and working her bundt off for you.